She Stood There
Laughing

She Stood There Laughing

A man, his son, and their football club

STEPHEN FOSTER

Scribner

First published in Great Britain by Scribner, 2004
An imprint of Simon & Schuster UK Ltd
A Viacom Company

Copyright © Stephen Foster, 2004

1 3 5 7 9 10 8 6 4 2

Simon & Schuster UK Ltd
Africa House
64–78 Kingsway
London WC2B 6AH

www.simonsays.co.uk

Simon & Schuster Australia
Sydney

A CIP catalogue record for this book is available from the British Library

ISBN 0-7432-5683-2

Typeset by M Rules
Printed and bound in Great Britain
by Cox & Wyman Ltd, Reading, Berks

For Carole

Acknowledgements

Thanks to: Arkwright, Arthur, Peter Balding, Bumble, Marion Catlin, Rosie Edwards, Graham Etherington, Mrs Etherington, Karen Fisk, Mr Fisk, Mark Finney, Marion Forsyth, Adam Groom, Henry, Jamilla, Jo-Jo, Adrian Lowery, Megan, Robert and Christopher and Andrew Moulton, Clair Myhill, Mick Norcop, Tony Norcop, Anjali Pratap, John Street, the Brandon-Streets, Sybil Smut, George Szirtes, Tommani, Theo, Clarissa Upchurch, Rochelle Venables, Diane Watson.

The massive: Tom Harvey, Tom Horan, Jack Jeffrey, Sam Johnson, Sam Martin, Andrew Muir, John Muir, Luke Richmond, Will Tuttle, Tom Wattam, Matthew Woodall.

Special thanks to:

Derek Johns at AP Watt for sorting the deal.
Tim Binding at Scribner for putting an offer in.
Ben Keane for learned advice on how to cut the crap.

Extra special thanks to Trezza Azzopardi for putting up with it, and much more.

*This is a record of a season
with our football club*

How it begins

It's an early start for the opening match back in the next-to-top flight.

But all starts are early for Jack and me, even for 'home' games, because Norwich, where we live, is in Norfolk, whereas Stoke is 200 miles away in Staffordshire. It's all right for me, it's explicable at least, seeing as I was born and brought up in the Potteries. As soon as I was old enough to catch buses on my own I would spend my pocket money, my extra earnings, and my whole Saturday at the Victoria Ground, the old stadium; getting there before the gates even opened in order to watch the teams arrive, and hanging around long after the match had finished in order to watch the television interviews being conducted on the pitch. If I have an idealized still of my childhood, it's of standing amongst a small group of like-minded boys beside the players' tunnel, as drizzle falls through the beam of the floodlights, waiting to see which one of the team will come out to talk to the presenter. It will most likely be a player that scored a goal, though they do give the defenders a go sometimes. On an absolutely perfect occasion, on completion of his work in front of camera, the player might autograph my programme and possibly ruffle my hair and maybe even refer to me as *mate*. Sometimes on a Sunday I'd bike down to the ground and circle its silence, reliving the day before.

1

Though I left Stoke years ago, Stoke has never left me, and Stoke City-related thoughts interrupt my every day. Football at large in its ever-present hum forms an abstract background to life: I turn to the back pages as a matter of instinct, my television and radio sets self-tune to live coverage – in this way the happenings of other teams detain and occupy me like rolling news. I'm able to admire, in a detached way, patterns of passing and moments of perfect skill in other sides; I'm vaguely capable of empathizing with what the supporters of those other sides might be going through in their high and low moments. But only vaguely, because when it comes to the goals – the acts that necessarily define those high and low moments – only the ones that Stoke City score have any meaning to me. In short, in the words of the song, I'm City til I die, because I was born that way.

For Jack, who has become in the past few seasons as much of a committed Stoke supporter as I am – owner of many replica shirts, a tatty wonky flag, and much more associated and unnecessary memorabilia besides (for example, he uses all of his devices to try to persuade me to part with a substantial amount of cash for a Stoke City signet-ring) – such dedication is more complex. He was born in Denmark Hill in London, and is therefore technically within his rights to follow Crystal Palace or Millwall. But he is a reasonably well-adjusted individual and supports neither. We moved to Norwich when he was one year old. In his early days he was a keen Norwich City aficionado and has actually cheered for the Canaries against Stoke when we've been in the same division. Sitting beside me on a horrible afternoon in 1995 for example, he was able, and entitled, to give it up in style as Norwich recorded their fastest *ever* goal at Carrow Road. It took ten seconds from the centre spot to the back of our net. Ho ho ho. Being the butt of stats like that is one of the services Stoke provide to football. Norwich '95 was, it goes without saying, a game that we went on to lose. Ha ha ha.

To lose a football match is normal. To lose one in this way is special:

I took Jack to see us play Liverpool in the Worthington Cup one winter's night at the beginning of the new millennium – less than a year, now I think of it, after his mum and I split up. We were annihilated 0–8 [eight] (as the old teleprinter would have been compelled to confirm it), a record home defeat, and a challenging situation for the scoreboard operator who actually had it down as 0–9 [nine]. Something happened that night. Something beyond the wonder of the scoreline. And that something was that Jack became mesmerized and entranced. Possibly by the epic-ness of the reverse, certainly by the ceaselessness of our support in the face of it. You wouldn't get that at Norwich, Dad, he said, in an effort to comfort me. He wasn't wrong. The default mode of the crowd at Carrow Road is set to silent-with-occasional-whinging, punctuated by pockets of silence. It was on leaving this match that, at his insistence, I purchased the first of Jack's replica shirts, of which there is now an extensive collection. And from that moment on, the overpriced purplish garment safely zipped within the folds of his hoody, his allegiance was transferred. Completely. That's the sort of boy he is. I counselled against it, of course; I'd have been abdicating my fatherly responsibility were it otherwise. It's lifelong pain, misery and despair you're looking at here, you do know that, don't you? I said. But you can't tell them when they're teenagers, they know best. Maybe I could have warned more vehemently. Not that it would've made any difference, with it being clear that his mind was set. But I didn't warn more vehemently because I was very proud of him indeed.

Soon after the transfer of affiliation was formalized (the replica shirt was worn in public out here on the Eastside) I was making calculations as to how this could affect my life, or, more accurately, our lives together. Taking him to see us play Liverpool was one thing, a 'treat'. But now, at last, I had an excuse to attend away matches at Peterborough, Colchester, Cambridge, Northampton – those tiny, archaic,[1] faintly tragic eastern counties grounds not so far from Norwich. Venues where the Mighty Potters should never be playing in the first place, and to which, had I travelled on my own, as was my desire, could only throw me into the light of being, as our ex-ex-manager would have put it, a sad twat. Sad no more. These wretched, yet oddly charming stadiums with their antediluvian terracing (a child of the Sky age, Jack had never seen such things: Wow, Dad, look at *this* – you *stand up!*) had suddenly become places to which I could share adventures with my son.

A magnificent result.

And so his allegiance bedded down, and we began to travel

---

1 Though Northampton's ground is newish, it still retains this flavour.

to more and more games, eventually seeing most of the fixtures in the 2001–02 season, a year that culminated in promotion. It was a difficult promotion filled with difficult times. Jack does not take kindly to journeying down to the badlands of Berkshire to see us lose 1–0 to Reading. Who the fucking hell are they? He has not yet developed the emotional armour to see us defeated at home by Tranmere, Queens Park Rangers (my generation may remember them as a proper club, his doesn't), or even – oh no, oh no, oh no, oh no – Port Vale, another football team from the Potteries, incomparably unattractive. All this comes as a huge blow to him, even if he does get to preview his hip-hop mixes to a captive audience (me) for the hours spent on the road there and back, trouser a fiver from his Gran-in-Stoke, and savour an exquisite diet of chips, mushy peas, Dr Peppers, meat pies and megabeans while he's at it. He needs more. His craving is the same as it is for every fan of every club: he's in it for the glory. It's an extraordinary condition of football-supporting – a condition to which the young are particularly vulnerable – that you only need to see your team win once[2] to instil the belief that this can happen every time they play. Like hoping to see the sun shine each morning when you wake, it's a wish that bears no relation to the harsh reality of the climate in Stoke-on-Trent.

---

2 It was a deceptively stylish *home* victory over who the fucking hell are Reading in Jack's case.

How it began

1972. A Saturday night. A country club just outside the south Cheshire village of Alsager. Beneath the mirror ball, in the fog of Panatella smoke, Stoke City players celebrate their victory of earlier in the day. Towards closing time – an idea that exists in law, but is fictional in practice, as the staff will serve for as long as there are Cinzanos to be drunk – Tony Waddington, the Stoke City manager, gives my mum the old, 'Would you like to come outside and see my car?' routine.

She thinks this will be safe enough. Tony is a charming, beatific, squiffy middle-aged gent, and so she accompanies him into the night air anticipating the class of motor she is about to examine. What might the boss of a top-flight football club drive? A Bentley? A Stag? A Lotus? A Rolls? An E-Type Jaguar maybe. Perhaps just a simple Daimler or Mercedes.

The car is an Austin Maxi.

1972.

1972 is a mythical year in our history because this is the year in which the team collect their first, and to date only, major trophy by beating Chelsea 2–1 in the League Cup Final. In 1972 I am a ticketless ten-year-old boy kicking a ball around a side passage, listening to the game on the radio, re-scoring our goals, as I picture them from the commentary, against a garage door. Stoke City Football Club are established 109 years prior to this cup triumph. The idea that the acquisition of such silverware is long overdue does not occur to me. It happens so early in my life, and sooner still into my football-supporting life, that it seems a straightforward matter: the club which represents my home city is the cup-winning kind of club. Securely established in the top division, it is a club that plays stylish football and has players of the kind you must be careful to protect from the predators who come hunting from Manchester in the North and from London in the South. Stoke have been to the FA Cup semi-finals in consecutive years as well as winning the League Cup. You cannot hide your light under a bushel in these circumstances. Transfer raids are not out of the question; they can, will, and do happen. They cause me fear and alarm. Still, I have to understand that there's a price to be paid for our level of success, a level of success which seems to me to be *normal*, and that attempts to steal my heroes is that price.

But the success is *not* normal. The class of 1972 are an historical abnormality who have never been surpassed or even nearly-equalled.

It is Tony Waddington who is responsible for this. Waddo is a great man, a great man who lives in a world of his own – a person who believes that he can impress the ladies by giving them a tour of a four-door saloon manufactured by British Leyland. He is clearly seeking an exacting challenge from this life, and he has found it. Calling on a talent that is little short of sorcery, he has managed to create an elegant football team where before there has been a clapped-out one. He has performed extraordinary feats: in tempting Stanley Matthews back to the club from Blackpool he has supplied the catalyst that fills the stadium to such a level that youths are to be seen perched halfway up the floodlight stanchions. The concept of Health and Safety has yet to be devised, and the re-appearance of the legendary winger in his proper shirt, our red and white stripes, finds so many extra supporters rammed into the ground that the attendance *quadruples*. Stan is well into his forties even then, and still plays for us at more than fifty years of age. Waddo persuades Alan Hudson, a footballing God from the Kings Road, that a life in the Potteries will suit him, and signs him for an English record-breaking transfer fee. He tries to lure Peter Osgood, Hudson's fellow Chelsea gunslinger, in a speculative two-for-one deal while he's at it. He fails to convince Osgood, but his verve in making the attempt slows me to a stop on my way back from picking up the *Evening Sentinel Late Final* as I follow the enthralling details of this extraordinary wheeler-dealing. Beside being enthralled, my specific fears are also being assuaged: it is *we* who are the transfer looters. It is *us* who must be feared by other clubs. My match days, if this is possible, are to be anticipated with even greater expectancy. My match days are the culmination of my life and I tell you they are fucking dangerous.

Getting yourself killed by gangs of bootboys outside before the match is a genuine prospect, and not getting yourself killed by them after the match is an accomplishment assisted by an intimate knowledge of the rat-runs through the terraced streets around the ground and a hundred-yard sprint-time provoked by fuel-injected adrenaline. My match days are spent on my toes on the vast terrace of the Boothen End, a small specimen in a crowd of the sort where, as a consequence of goal celebrations, I will find myself turned upside down thirty feet from where I began, in a pool of piss. Not everyone bothers to use the toilet at half-time, some urinate where they stand, the dirty bastards (though the Gents itself *is* unsavoury in that it features a deep end and a shallow end). The air is ripe with the stench of beer and fags and sweat, and the language is equally foul: this is living; this is what life is for. I know it in my bones and I adore it. The team, which I adore most of all, win games with flair and are all fit to play alongside England's finest ever goalkeeper, *our* goalkeeper, Gordon Banks, a World Cup winner who is famous across the planet for making the greatest save of all time against Pele of Brazil. This is our Golden Age, these are the years when we are given pride and allowed to feel like champions.

The Golden Age

. . . was a blip, a statistical anomaly, an accident. Those few seasons that coincided with my football induction now seem like tricks of the mind, made possible only because we were managed by a gifted one who ran the team according to a vision of greatness. As you grow up you realize the distasteful truth that the business of a football club cannot continue like this indefinitely. With the team fading as the seventies were looking towards the eighties, Tony departed, dematerialized, and the magic went with him. Those that he left behind were not blessed with his gift, absolutely the reverse, and our post-Waddington decline has been permanent. Life has never been anything like the same since.

But, to alter the maths and to add a rider to an old saying: Give me the boy until he's a ten-year-old following a football team, and I'll give you the man. I've never been anything like the same since either. As I passed by and nodded at the wisdom and beauty of graffiti which read *The Wad Is God*, how could I possibly know that for the first and last time I was experiencing unblemished personal happiness? I vividly recall, in the early nineties (when we had been dreadful, and more often pitiful, for well over a decade) reading *Fever Pitch*, Nick Hornby's chronicle of the life and sorry times of an Arsenal fan. My knee-jerk response to this book was, You lucky, lucky bastard. Wrapped in my own misery, I had never considered what people who follow genuinely successful teams might be like. They'd have it better than me, surely? But football fans are born whingers, and I had to laugh as Hornby bemoaned his lot as the seasons turned bad, as the Gunners just missed out on the Championship or only came runners-up in the FA Cup Final one more time. Getting to the FA Cup Final would be a first for Stoke. For us a bad season involves changing manager three times, losing to Port Vale both home and away (*fixtures* that would have been unthinkable in 1972, never mind the results), selling our top scorer to a team worse than ourselves, getting knocked out of the FA Cup before Bonfire

Night, getting knocked out of all other knockout competitions even earlier, being rolled 6–0 by Swindon Town, and finishing up relegated to the Second (old Third) Division.

And to add to it, the bad season is the usual season. Post-Waddington, all the way to the present day – a quarter of a century – the bad season is the state of affairs that now comes to categorize and define my use of the word *normal*.

It's routine to hear football described as a religion. I feel more afflicted than anointed. From what I hear on radio phone-ins, in the moments of conversation I share with the supporters of our opponents, and from looking in on fanzines and online messageboards and the like, mine is hardly a unique perception. All the same, hundreds of thousands of us dedicate untold hours of our lives, and whatever it is we hold in our secular souls, to the following of our underperforming, underachieving teams, paying our weekly respects at the altar of disappointment. Why?

In the mid-eighties, when we were at our worst and I was an angry young man operating one of my several post-Waddington Stoke City boycotts, I began an austere phase, spending afternoons on my bed reading books I thought would be good for me. George Orwell was a favourite. I remember slowing on a comment he made about the refuelling habits of industrial employees in the North of England: he observed that the working classes didn't care whether smoking cigarettes and eating jam butties was good for them or not, they did it for enjoyment, for the respite it afforded them from the rest of life. They did it for pleasure. I drew on my fag in silent accord. If the physical nature of work and the material world is wildly different now to the way it was in Orwell's time, most of us are nonetheless familiar with a predictable pattern of work and bills and responsibility. A jam butty is still a treat; a Saturday afternoon at a match is still time out from the routine, and, like a cigarette, it's a habit as well as a comfort as well as a killer. Any team *can* occasionally transcend the mundane, produce the back-heel or the volley or the bicycle-kick which, if only momentarily, transports us elsewhere and allows us to feel beloved. Prior to kick-off our team is *always* capable of delivering the sweet taste of victory. It is my belief that the nature of our affliction is to be addicted to this: to a capability, to a possibility; to a *prospect*. I closed *The Road to Wigan Pier* and I went to the game.

However. There's often a great deal less pleasure involved in football than in a jam butty or a Marlboro Light. If it's not quite sado-masochistic to devote so much of our*selves* to it – to the chance that the average players participating in the average spectacle might actually *win* for *us* – more often than not we wouldn't describe it as a joy either. So what is the pay-off? What is the majority, non-Arsenal, non-Man United, non-Premiership football-supporter's habitual state? It is the (more or less vain) anticipation of not being unjoyful at the end of ninety minutes. That's the best most of us can hope for.

Stoke City Syndrome is a specific and particularly virulent mutation of the condition. Really, I should be sorry for what I have done in exacerbating the matter by handing the disorder on to my son (though the circumstances of his infection could not possibly have been predicted). Still, had I considered it properly, I might have thought better than to take him to a full house against the Scousers. We would not show them we cared about the humiliating loss; we would not confess it: that was the ceaselessness of the support. For the impressionable, we are a potent crowd – pockets of silence are not our thing. Stoke-on-Trent is a very poor city, and as in many such areas its people are possessed of a seductive low-rent charm and the chip-on-shoulder which most naturally translate into rough self-protective humour. I should never have taken him in amongst us. He was at an age and at a point where he was open to falling for the idea that *this* could be him, that *he* could be this.

The pre-season: the iceman cometh a cropper

May, 2002. Thirty years after the Golden Age.

Three grown men in replica shirts and jeans sit on the staircase of the Angel Hotel opposite the Millennium Stadium in Cardiff in complete silence, heads hanging, shoulders drooped, pints dangling, a picture of abject despondence. An hour earlier, across the road, their team has been promoted in a play-off final.

Come on lads, I say, passing between them. Lighten up: we won. We've gone up!

It's too much to take in, one replies, without making any improvement to his body language. His colleagues, if they make any response whatsoever, may nod their agreement, though I couldn't be sure.

Jack leads me up the flight as we pass between them. Though it is my urgent desire to secure a pint of my own to dangle, we must first perform his mission: to hang the tatty red and white flag with the club crest and the word 'Potters' from our room window. The club crest slopes off-centre; the word Potters is printed on the wonk. He'd purchased the flag from a street vendor earlier in the day, the last of its type. It's already more than a souvenir, it's a collector's item, but, notwithstanding this, we must risk its rarity value by draping it from the Angel's façade for all the world to recognize and acknowledge.

Stoke City had spent the season prior to this play-off final in the Second Division of the Nationwide League for the fourth year running. We had been relegated along with Manchester City in 1998, City beating us 5–2 in the final game, a result which wasn't enough to save them, and which neatly summed us up. We were the kind of hopeless losers who weren't even capable of mustering enough pride not to ship five goals against another bunch of hopeless losers on the last day of a truly miserable life. It had been a dismal campaign, if that word could in any sense be applied to the activities that had taken place during a season in which we had given work to one dire manager after another. In the way that these things often go, each dire incumbent had club connections while none had a remotely plausible employment record. We recorded our heaviest ever home *League* defeat 0–7 [seven] (as the old teleprinter would once more have been compelled to confirm) to Birmingham City. *Birmingham City.* As one of the original members of the Football League we had waited over a century to see a thing as unspeakable as this, and it was tempting to regard it as an achievement. For some of our followers, however, the store of black humour required to view the result in such a light was long depleted. By smashing the place up at the final whistle, they secured a response of sorts: in the following days, one of the dire managers was exchanged for another. While Manchester City revived themselves in their own specialized manner, bouncing straight back up out of the Second Division and onwards, Stoke supporters suffered the first of the four relegated seasons under another new manager, this one not club-connected, but nonetheless from another recognizable category of direness: the dreary, hopeless case. The announcement of his appointment was news of the type that makes your heart sink. He was called Brian Little. We finished in his image – in a nondescript position outside the play-off zone. Thankfully he quit after merely the one deathly year in charge, looking like he'd had some kind of breakdown. Perhaps he'd just bored himself to death, like he had us.

Lying fourth from top and playing solidly (if not a little stolidly) under the next new manager, Gary Megson, a third of the way into the second of our relegated seasons, the sitting board made the unique decision to sell the club to a collective of Icelandic businessmen. It is a comment on the record of those sitting board members that this didn't strike anyone as an especially terrible idea. A company called Stoke Holding was registered in Luxembourg. The directors of this firm were an assemblage of individuals who'd made money from various trades including, unsurprisingly, trawler-fishing. Megson was dismissed as the travellers from the land of ice and fire delivered their own manager.

Gudjon Thordarson had previously been in charge of the Icelandic national team. If you overlooked the fact that Iceland's world ranking averages at about the same level as Israel's, this didn't sound entirely unimpressive, particularly in the light of our recent past. In his first two seasons Gudjon (quickly known as Mr G – Gudjon being considered a dubious word to pronounce amongst many Potters) took the club to the play-offs where each time we lost in the semi-final. On the first occasion it was down to the refs: the home ref with his mystery five minutes of added time which enabled Gillingham to score – in the mystery *sixth* minute of added time – an away goal that would prove to be vital. The ref at their place was a good deal worse (he would be, he was Rob Styles), deciding to guarantee Gills a victory by sending off two of our players early in the game. Even with just nine men we still forced the extra period, but by then we were knackered out and the rigged match was lost 0–3.

The following year we played Walsall in the play-off semis. A goalless draw at home was followed by a Gudjon Awayday Special. By now we'd seen this too often before. Mr G displayed his Achilles' heel at Walsall: his Achilles' heel was 5–3–2. If it was beyond the imagination of the squad to comprehend what 5–3–2 was supposed to mean – and it was – by now we understood it too well. It meant defeat, preceded by a shambles, which is exactly what we got. And for total accuracy, and added shambolicity, a 5–4–1 system with many normal positions redistributed was given a world première that night. It was a formation that was as novel to us as it was to the players, who, charting new areas on the field of play, were as disorientated as any sane person would expect them to be. It was an unbelievable moment for a manager to go in for a game of poker. I think it was 4–1 we lost. I try to forget.

And so the humiliation of seeing the Rip-Roaring Mighty Potters playing at semi-derelict venues where our support put a tremendous supplement on the normal gate – Colchester United for example – continued, while our rendition of our anthem, Tom Jones' 'Delilah'[3] –

I saw the light on the night that I passed by her window:
Whoawhoawhoawhoa,
I saw the flickering shadows of love on her blind:
Whoawhoawhoawhoa . . .

– put a tremendous supplement on the atmosphere.

*

---

3 A tradition originating from a pub juke-box one night in the eighties. Some of our rowdies were singing crude songs and a policeman asked them if they could restrict themselves to cleaner lyrics. 'Delilah' was the next track on. It stuck. Why? (why why

We don't play in a dilapidated old shed ourselves: we are a big club with a new address. In 1997 we moved to the Britannia Stadium where 28,000 supporters can be seated in comfort. In some sort of physical comfort anyway. So far as mental well-being is concerned, that's a different matter. The Britannia is built half-way up a hill in the shadow of the municipal incinerator. As architectural metaphors go it's just about perfect: our relegation alongside Manchester City saw us drop a division in our first season there.

Even in the light of the Walsall experiment, Gudjon was afforded a last chance. One of his best players, Graham Kavanagh, was sold in the close season for a million to Cardiff but Mr G was allowed to re-invest some of the money from this sale, and five cut-price replacements arrived. Amongst these was the Dutchman Peter Hoekstra, who had a running style akin to a delicate, slightly damaged swan and played, when uninjured which wasn't often, like Cruyff's talented younger brother. Highly irregular. We are more used to the likes of another international who came as part of this package, Sergei Shtaniuk: combative, utilitarian Serge turned out to be a natural crowd pleaser and had us watching out for the international results of Belorussia.

Gudjon's last chance got off to a patchy start. Just a few

---

why?) Because it's an anthem of defiance in the face of distress. Our interpretation has developed into a perfectly rehearsed version based on call-and-response, whereby a madman will sing lines one and three and the crowd take the rest.

games in Mr G was once more forced to watch a player go to the Welsh capital. This time it was top scorer Peter Thorne for nearly two million, in order that we might pay the wage bill for the rest of the staff for the remainder of the year. This was a deal which enlightened us further, as if we needed it, as to how three seasons in the Second Division had affected the balance sheet. Animosity between Stoke City and Cardiff City supporters pre-existed these transactions. There had been over a hundred arrests at a match between the sides a couple of years earlier. It is not a geographical rivalry between the two sets of fans as most football hostilities tend to be, Cardiff being miles away and located in another principality: it's to do with who has the hardest hooligans (we do). In the light of this, seeing them nick our star players was not an example of emollient diplomacy. All of this dirty business meant that Jack was reviling Cardiff before he had ever even set foot in the place or seen them play.

In May, the normal league season concluded with Cardiff finishing a place ahead of Stoke, who were fifth. Automatic promotion had eluded us for the fourth year in succession. Once more it was the play-offs: the teams met over two extravagantly-policed semi-finals. Cardiff beat us 2–1 at the Britannia. For fuck's sake. It was goalless with the ninety minutes all but up at Ninian Park, the home crowd prematurely celebrating reaching the final, when our midfielder James O'Connor[4] produced something we'd seen precious little

---

4   Little Ginge, as his sponsors in the *Southern Potters Fanzine* quaintly termed him, as if, in a previous life, he flew alongside Biggles.

of from him prior to that night: a goal. He volleyed home, superbly nutmegging the aforementioned Kavanagh on the way, to bring the scores level over the two games. Nail me sideways. Here we had a thoroughly unexpected adjustment to the climate of despair.

In the extra period that followed the superb nutmegging, the same player took a free-kick from a few yards outside the penalty area. This is not normally his job, but then, these were not normal circumstances. It was quite, quite obvious where he was going to hit it and the keeper had the top corner covered. But, ingenuously, O'Connor had in mind a scheme involving Souleymane Oulare. Souleymane was a substitute who had played no part in the ninety minutes of normal time and who was making his second ever (and as it happened, last) appearance for us. His absence over the preceding months had been due to a life-threatening blood clot he'd developed on his lung immediately after we'd signed him from an obscure location in Belgium earlier in the year. Anyway, there he was, Souleymane, in the box. And there was O'Connor with his obvious-looking run-up. How could anyone have guessed that his free-kick scheme involved deflecting the ball into the Cardiff goal off Souleymane's arse? They could not. It was a device which worked brilliantly, totally wrong-footing not only all those watching but also – and most vitally – the Cardiff keeper. And after that, in the remaining ten minutes, we managed *not* to concede a pathetic equalizer and it was *Cardiff* who had the player sent off. Final score over the two legs was 3–2. To *us*. Utterly untypical-Stoke. Unheard of, unbelievable and extraordinary. It has become a given fact of existence that luck like this does not apply to our team. Dealing with life-threatening illnesses, reading out the injury-list, and selling our star performers to deadly rivals is the daily business of the club.

Normally we never, ever have any good fortune whatsoever. We're *fam*ous for not having it.

Normally, as at Gillingham, it's us who are down to ten men and on the receiving end of the last-minute equalizer and moments later down to nine men and on the receiving end of the fluke extra-time winner.

Normally, in the post-Waddo working definition of *normally*, normally one way or another, we lose.

Souleymane Oulare was a ten-minute hero before making a mystery disappearance back to the obscure Belgian location whence he came. He was never seen near Stoke ever again. His shorts sold for a record price in an auction a few weeks later.

While this remarkable play-off activity was taking place on a Wednesday night in south Wales, I was sitting beside some railway arches in my car outside a friend's house on the Eastside of England, in a suburb of Norwich. I was supposed to be having dinner with the friends, but I was a very poor guest who would never have accepted the invitation in the first place if he'd properly consulted his diary. I'd already taken their kitchen radio and tuned it into BBC Radio Five Live, turned it down low and put it between my feet under the table. During the main course I contributed nothing to the conversation, having my ear out for score updates (the commentary was from some other match, naturally) and resigning myself, as the minutes passed away, to defeat as per the bleedin' norm. O'Connor's late equalizer saw me leaping out of my chair cheering and yelping and knocking wine glasses over. The broadcasters at least had the decency to switch to full coverage for the extra time. I apologized and excused myself. In the car, I could at least give the situation the undivided attention it demanded and also have a fag without getting told off. On the note of the final whistle my phone rang. Jack had already bollocked me for making the stupid dinner arrangement. But the match was *not* televised.

Would listening to the radio together help us, d'you think, I had asked him.

He said nothing in response to this question, the sort of nothing that is a silent accusation.

So he had listened to it at home, at his mum's. Jack is fourteen. He was making this noise down the earpiece:

YEEEEEEESSSSSSSSSSSSSSSSSSSSSSSSAAAAARRRRGGGGGGHHHHHH!!!

I replied in kind.

When we stopped, he said, We'll get tickets for the final, Dad, won't we?

Don't worry about that mate.

We had been to the first leg, and we were more than hacked-off that we hadn't made it cross-country right there and then, though it would have been trickier to get to than even the distance involved dictated because policing requirements meant that we'd only have been allowed into Ninian Park on an official club coach, so we'd have had to travel from Norwich to Wales via Stoke to see the game, and back the same way. You can get to Italy quicker and cheaper.

In defeating the Cardiff scum, the knock-on effect was that Mr G had ensured his job security, which had been under question for a while, never more so than in those last few minutes of normal time at Ninian Park, at least until the final. Thirty-five thousand Stokies made the trip to the Millennium Stadium, where the tatty wonky flag which now forms the centrepiece to Jack's Stoke Wall of Fame in the bedroom he keeps at our place was acquired. We won the match comfortably, improving on a recent lousy losing League display against Brentford by beating them 2–0. *Brentford.* I ask you.

Less than a week after this victory the club made the unexpected announcement that the manager had been sacked because his position was untenable. For a few days 'untenable' became the buzzword of buzzwords in the Potteries. Some claimed to know the full untenability of Gudjon's position, while others failed to understand why it was that his position was untenable at all given that he'd fulfilled his obligations and finally at long last got us up. Many took the view that this achievement could imply that he ought to be given the chance to test his talents at the higher level. However, finding himself in an untenable situation, that was no longer a possibility.

If the question of tenability remained an issue for some time (it did) one matter was more certain. In sacking their own man in such circumstances the Icelandics were demonstrating a respect for the legacy of generations of Stoke City board members. In paving the way for a period of unrest that very few clubs can accomplish in the aftermath of a triumph, they were ensuring that the moment was tainted with the essence of fiasco without which it might not be complete. Gudjon himself had been instrumental in bringing about the buyout, and was unquestionably the figurehead of the owners. It was in his capacity as national coach, while watching big Larus Sigurdsson lump the ball out of defence for us, that he became aware of the financial vulnerability (or potential, if you prefer) of the SCFC operation. He was entitled to feel more than aggrieved at this unseemly development. Through the website of our fanzine, *The Oatcake*,[5] a demo was organized at the stadium in favour of Mr G's re-employment. If it was obvious before this assembly that there would be no way back – a re-instatement of this nature would be unprecedented in professional football – it was even clearer after it: Mr G addressed this meeting himself, referring to his erstwhile colleagues as 'fucking twats'. While rumour and counter-rumour circulated concerning the nature of the deterioration of his relationship with the

---

5   Named after the local delicacy. Not to be confused with the (impostor) dry Scottish biscuit. The Staffordshire oatcake is floppy and pancake-like, usually rolled and served warm with a variety of sweet or savoury fillings, and cold on cocktail sticks at parties.

consortium of twats, the indisputable side-effect was that the treatment he received took the shine off the promotion for a great many supporters. What might have been a lengthy party lasted just the four days it took for the fiasco to become public and the recriminations to begin. A measure of stability might not have seemed an unreasonable concept for a squad which, despite being deprived of its star players, had scraped its way up a division. But stability is a notion with which the club prefer to remain unfamiliar.

Still:

The New Season

will always begin again:

Summertime

and the living is easier than it would be if we were looking at a filthy fifth year in the Second Division. Whatever else we were all disputing, we could find easy consensus on that.

At last, we were back in the big time, playing at a level where we believe we belong. As a matter of fact, if we're completely open, we believe we should be in the Premiership. We do after all have a triptychal statue of the late Sir Stan outside the ground to remind us of what we once were. We do after all have the *memory* of being competitors. A remarkable number of forty-odd-year-olds attend our games, supporters who were ten-year-olds at the same time I was. I see them trailing their children behind them, feeding them tales of glory nights of cup draws against Ajax of Amsterdam, neglecting to mention shameful third-round days of getting knocked out of the FA Cup by Blyth Spartans. For us at least, and maybe even for the trailing child, we were able to get worked up as we studied a fixture list which, instead of cataloguing a sequence of misery visits to the likes of Layer Road and Vale Park, took in the glamour of Molineux and the venue to which the first early start of the new term delivers us.

Hillsborough

As we arrive into Sheffield from the east, we're chuffed to see how many of us have piled in from the Potteries. The team that achieves promotion through the play-offs enjoys an extra wash of enthusiasm for the new existence in the higher division, the lifeline having come so late in the day, the memory of the escape so vivid. We were more than relieved simply to be there at all. Other questions occupied our minds: Could our boys cut it at this level? What style would we be playing under the new manager? (a question which is seldom far from our lips.) How will the close-season signings shape up? Any hope of improved catering?

While it's a racing certainty that the answer to the last will be No – and chip butties in Hillsborough's West Stand were already off the carte half an hour before kick-off, leaving a flat choice between a chicken balti pie or a Yorkie – the answers to the other questions occupy many of our waking thoughts.

As we've only made one close season signing – striker Chris Greenacre on a free, prolific scorer in the Third Division with Mansfield Town, who, in the time-honoured Stoke-new-signing-tradition, has hurt himself in a friendly – then the whole weight of close-season signing anticipation rests on his young shoulders and injured ankle. Greenacre will either recover and score goals, in which case we'll sell him, or he won't, in which case we won't be able to sell him. Football fans fall into two broad categories, the blind optimists and the doom-mongerers. If he doesn't score goals the optimists will say that he just needs a break, that he's a *trier*. And then they will bring out their pet word and say that he is *honest*. Honest is my least favourite cliché in football; Honest is a euphemism for Useless. I've noticed that jockeys often use the word to describe their mount prior to saddling a horse that comes home twelfth: *Ah to be sure he's a very genuine honest animal*. The doom-mongerers will employ predictably industrial language, describing him as a total fucking waste of space, time and money, but, since he came for nothing, will have to correct themselves and make do with simply a total fucking waste of space and time, which doesn't have the right nailed-on ring to it. If only the club could see their way to actually *purchasing* a striker, that would at least assist when it came to abusing the hopeless tosser.

Anyway, injured as Greenacre is, for the time being he's a prospect. And he scored a hat-trick too, in another friendly, prior to the injury-friendly. So we can make that a *great* prospect.

As to our new coach and his possible playing style – well, before getting started on him, a few words about the departed Gudjon. Unless a manager is universally hated by the support (Alan Ball) then his departure is, at some level, akin to the loss of a father. If Gudjon was a flawed patriarch, which he was – remote, difficult to read, short, sometimes bearded, always Icelandic, often tactically inept, not to mention an embarrassment to be seen out with: a manager of the tracksuit-wearing school, wholly unkempt, reminiscent of a park-team coach – he was nonetheless possessed of a certain aloof calm. This made for an oddly reassuring atmosphere about his person as he leant scruffily on the corner of the dugout in his beanie during matches, remaining unflappable and enigmatic even in the light of the unhappy events taking place before his very eyes and in his name. Apparently he was bad-tempered and cantankerous behind the scenes and dissent in the ranks was the order of the day, but his public face never revealed that, or anything else much, until the moment his colleagues on the board betrayed him. He could do nothing to hide his dismay as, shortly after hearing the news himself, we saw his devastated expression on our televisions. He was evidently shattered, and the pictures earned him even more of our sympathy than he might otherwise have received. In short, he looked a Stokie. We'll miss him, I think. The uncertainty of his team selections and playing formations made for a life that, if largely miserable, was seldom dull: misery we can live with, it's the tedium that does you in.

Post-Mr G, speculation was the name of the game. Those touted as the most likely in the race to replace formed an unpromising collection of the unemployed, the unemployable and litigants (Bruce Grobbelaar sent in a CV). From this worrying list, a rather more junior applicant ended up with the job. Steve Cotterill was a young manager who'd taken Cheltenham Town from the non-League to the Second Division in the past few seasons. In the worst-case scenario, the one that so nearly came about but for O'Connor's contributions at Ninian Park, we'd actually have been playing Cheltenham Town this year. *In the League.* Quite unthinkable. The only way such a fixture should be possible is by us losing to them in the third round of the FA Cup.

Cotterill's accomplishments in Gloucestershire were achieved on next-to-no money: for this reason alone you could see the sense in his appointment. The 2002–03 season followed the collapse of the Football League's television deal with broadcasters ITV Digital, which meant that the financial rewards we could have expected to receive as a result of the promotion were wiped out. Typical, and precisely what we didn't need; any study on any measure of countrywide wealth-distribution will produce a table that has Stoke-on-Trent propping it up. Conversely, any table of bad things will have Stoke topping it: for instance, we have the most fatties per head of population, the highest incidence of mobile phone deception, the lowest life expectancy in adult males. Et cetera. For a variety of reasons, all of them attributable to the second-rate complacents charged with running things – the Pottery Barons and the like who have a vested interest in maintaining the feudal system – the city is nowhere near post-industrial recovery. And the football club is not exempt from the general picture.

So, if we didn't know much about our new stepfather – *Steve who?* – we'd at least heard that he'd proved himself capable of moulding one successful team on a reduced budget, and for that we could allow ourselves guarded optimism. If, as it turned out when we first set eyes on him, he had the naturally pensive look of Lance, Paul Whitehouse's fishmonger sidekick to Harry Enfield's television stallholder, and big sticky-out ears to go with it, this was only of concern to us if such a pensive big-earedness were to to be translated into a negative style of play. Which was not out of the question, was it? He could take a look around, note that we sold and did not replace our top striker eons ago, that goals were hardly in abundant supply last season, and that our striker stand-ins and strikers-in-waiting appeared to be inadequate and at the same time working a shift system for picking up injuries. He could then ask the board for some money. After being turned down he could decide that the only way we could remain in the First Division would be by employing a wholly defensive game. Please, *anything* but that. Because not even those deranged persons who follow The Fail (Port Vale) want to pay to watch football of that type. (Or do they?) Surely not. All fans, with the exception of those singular cases who take their pleasures in dourness, want to see nine-goal thrillers in which their team triumphs 5–4. We're in it for the cut and for the thrust, for the tension and the tears and the *drama*. We're not in it for the five-man back line and the competently executed offside trap, because that restricted attitude represents the normal limitations of the everyday life from which we are seeking remove.

But even if all this is true, on the opening afternoon in the Yorkshire sunshine we were happy just to see Cotterill's selected XI avoid defeat, to evade a good playground-kicking by the nasty bullies from the year above. As a consequence of this heightened anxiety on behalf of our boys, contrary to the normal condition of football-supporting, the 6,000 of us who assembled on the blue seats of the North Stand probably *didn't* demand a win. In this mindset, the goalless draw we saw, with Stoke battling away and looking, well, no worse than the opposition – buttock-clenchingly tense as it was for the final eighty-five minutes – could easily be regarded as a victory. And our enthusiasm knew no bounds. When on our travels we have the simplest of all songs with which to answer the perennial enquiry put by the home support: Who are yer?

We are Stoke We are Stoke We are Stoke
We are Stoke We are Stoke We are Stoke
We are Stoke We are Stoke We are Stoke
We are STOKE
WE ARE STOKE

and we employed it to maximum sonic effect, handsomely and numerously turned out as we were on the first day of a new term.

On the couch

Leicester in midweek followed Sheffield, a live Sky match.[6] We stayed put in Norwich and watched it on television. It's so unusual for us to feature on the box, it's almost worth stopping in just so we can see what our players really look like in close-up: I have a far clearer picture of Roy Keane, for instance, that I do of Brynjar Gunnarsson. Don't we all. Fresh from relegation from the Premiership, Leicester looked one-dimensional and lifeless in winning 1–0 and we were a good second-best to that. You couldn't ask for a more graphic illustration of how the previous television deal collapsed: even supporters of the clubs involved would have trouble remaining glued to this dross, especially when at the touch of a button you could see Man United being beaten by some unheard-of Hungarians over on the BBC. The thought that outsiders might be watching us make a show of ourselves – we

---

6   A new broadcasting arrangement had been made. Sky paid peanuts. Had we have been promoted the season before we could have expected something like £1.75 million from television. Under this deal we could count ourselves lucky to pick up £350,000.

played in a clueless manner – was embarrassing. Our crowd turnout was low. Altogether, it was nothing to write home about.

'Fucking hell,' I said to Jack.

'What?'

'Rubbish isn't it?'

'Pass the sauce, Dad,' he replied. 'It's not that bad.'

The nature of our injury list hadn't changed just because we'd got a new manager, and the squad had been heavily trimmed in the summer too with some fringe players having been returned back to the Finnish third division. As a consequence we had several youngsters from the academy on the field. Jack's empathy was attracted to these boys, I think, who looked scarcely older than he did. One of them, Brian Wilson, a flyweight who'd struggle to gain admission into a '15' at the cinema, came on as sub. As the camera lingered on his worried little face, fellow exiled Stokie Graham Etherington sitting beside me on the sofa in his replica shirt, was moved to remark that he 'looked like he'd just been sent out for a loaf of bread.' He wasn't bad though, even if it was well past his bedtime. And another babyface, Kris Commons, on the left side, was putting on a one-man-show involving a catholic repertoire of skills, energy and talent, generally looking far too good, and redeeming us more than a little.

If Commons was the compensation in a crappy display, his performance provided the discompensation as well. He had supplied a top-up dose of the recurrent neurosis: how long before we sell him to Cardiff?

Still: two matches in, one point from a possible six. Could be worse.

Chasing losses

The season starts so early nowadays[7] that school has barely broken up for the summer as the opening fixtures kick off. The first match, the superb goalless draw from which we have our single point to date, took place when the holidays had just about begun. Bradford City visit our place a week later. We can't make it to this one as it is approaching the middle of the recess and Jack is leaving for Spain for a fortnight with his mum. After seeing him off, I make soup while listening to Premiership commentary on Five Live. An exiled supporter can follow his team's progress on the internet these days, but, unless the computer is in the kitchen, it's difficult to make soup at the same time, and for the ninety minutes that a match is on and you aren't at it, distractions like soup-making are more comforting than sitting chewing your nails and playing with your spinning-top while staring at the computer screen. Updates from other games – goals, sendings off – punctuate the action from the main commentary. As back-up I have the TV

---

7   Use of the word 'Nowadays' will elicit this response: You're an OLD MAN, Dad, things was different when you was young wasn't they and all you got for Christmas was a lump of coal, yawn, yawn, *yawn*.

switched to Teletext in the next room. You can't rely on just a single source. I was much more excited than should be possible when I first tuned into Teletext this season and realized that by moving up a division we'd been promoted on text too, from page 307 to page 305. Although I knew this would happen, I hadn't thought about it until I saw it. Not thinking about it until I saw it is the kind of oversight that my partner, Trezza, would describe as a small mercy in the life of a sad twat. Midway through the first half of whichever boring Premiership match it was they were at, there was a splash from the pan as the commentary team cut away to advise that someone called Andrew Cook had put us one up. Cookie! I shouted. Cookie!! Cookie!!![8] Trezza didn't trouble herself to check what was up, nor did she think I was praising myself vis-à-vis my *potage de légumes*. She knows.

But yet, even though we've scored our first goal of the season, I'm slighted. Andrew? Nobody calls him that. Even if you're being formal it's Andy. Typical. At the BBC, they don't even know who our players are. His name is Cookie.

By half-time it's 2–0. I stand staring at page 305. Well. Well well well.

GOOAARRRNNN.

And it stays that way until Bradford pull one back after the ninetieth minute. Final score 2–1. Our first win. We'll be safe in

---

8   Though an Honest striker, Cookie is a Stokle. He's the only one of our team who is local and supported us as a boy. That *does* weigh in significantly as a balance against his Honesty.

mid-table on page 325 in a minute or so, when they've adjusted it for today's results. The only cloud on my horizon, and let's face it, this should be an entirely cloud-free moment, is that in an effort to recover reverses I'd suffered at Newmarket the night before, I had been forced to stop off at William Hill to predict a final score of 2–0 at odds of 15–2. So, as a consequence of the losing betting slip tucked inside the pocket of my soup-spattered apron, there I am feeling pissed-off when I should be experiencing only pleasure and relief. Pathetic. And to make it worse, to say I was trying to recover Newmarket losses is, at best, a partial explanation, more like a damn fib, and goes against the first rule of gambling – when you've blown it, walk. *No Chasing*. It's thrill-seeking, that's all it really is, a lame effort at compensating for not experiencing the visceral kick of being at the match. It simply puts extra stress on something that's already too stressful, as if life isn't hazardous enough as it is with eating jam butties, driving to football grounds situated in dangerous locations like Colchester, and smoking. I've given up smoking which means I only sneak a small number of roll-ups, though never in front of Jack as no pleasure is possible under his gaze of disapproval.

Still: three matches, four points, only ten quid down. The season is shaping up nice.

36

The road to Preston North End

Even to me it seems perverse to drive 250 miles west when the match of the day is taking place two and a half minute's walk from home – Norwich entertaining the mighty Gillingham in one of those unfeasible top-versus-second fixtures you get when League tables are prepared after only three games. I'd been offered a free for this encounter. Given that I've already had to miss Bradford and only watched Leicester on telly (which doesn't count) I turned the free down, naturally, without a second's hesitation. In fact, I turned it down before the offerer even got his offer in. Feeling rude and ill-mannered about declining with such haste, I apologized by mentioning that I imagined the coast-to-coast journey I'd be making to Lancashire would lead me to watch a crappier contest. With Jack still in Spain I arrived alone at Deepdale, Preston's place, with half an hour to spare, which at least addressed one of my side-fears – that I'd miss kick-off. It's a usual concern when even home matches are away: roadworks, accidents, breakdowns, diversions, jams, iniquitous and vile one-way systems, the widening of the A11, more roadworks and diversions round the contraflows are all out there waiting to ruin the big day. Not to mention Acts of God . . .

A detour

I recall our despair when we heard on the radio halfway to Peterborough last year that the match had been called off due to a waterlogged pitch. We pulled into a petrol station and assessed the situation. Ipswich were playing Arsenal. Portman Road was within reach, and Jack nominated Arsenal as his Premiership club. I had a poor signal on my phone so we were allowed to call the Ipswich box office with *his* mobile on the understanding that I would be reimbursing him with a top-up voucher. They had two tickets remaining, each immediately behind a stanchion in different parts of the ground. This was an offer we could happily reject.

Aston Villa are at home, we could just about make it to Villa Park for three o'clock, I suggested.

Jack made the face he makes if you offer him mushrooms.

They've got that Juan Pablo Angel playing for them, I said.

Let's just turn round, shall we, he replied, which was unquestionably the right answer, unquestionably the only answer (and, for the record, don't think *I* wanted to watch Arsenal, much less Villa. I was only trying to help him out).

He went into a decline that I could understand all too well, and was powerless to repair. When you've got a game in your sights – which is the case for the whole of your life with the exception of those interminable weekends given over to internationals and the small window in the close season before the friendlies begin – your entire week builds towards it. You monitor your injury list on a daily basis. You check the opposition to see if they've got anyone decent playing for them – a quite unnecessary waste of time when you're in the Second Division. You study the table. You assess comparative home and away form. You look at the goal difference. You assess comparative home and away goal difference. Actually, you memorize the table. And you talk about it, a lot.[9]

Come the day you fill your thermos, you make the jam butties, you drape your backseat headrests with a scarf, you double-treble-check you've got tickets, credit cards, phone, specs, shades. Tickets. To be precise, you're in and out the house seven times before you're confident enough to start the engine. You start the engine. You insert the hip-hop tape. You quadruple check the tickets. You head out towards the ever-wider A11.

Your anticipation-trembles as kick-off time approaches are soothed only by the regularity of your routine: after the hip-hop, Five Live's matchday build-up, switching to Radio Stoke towards the ground and Thin Lizzy's 'The Boys Are Back In Town' on a special pre-match non-hip-hop tape as you reach

---

9 You're in constant struggle with yourself not to become a total bore. I remember hearing a story some years ago, told to me by a journalist whose house I was decorating, about him having John Motson, the football commentator, round for dinner. He said he was amazed by how one-dimensional Motson was, that whenever the topic veered away from Motty's specialist subject, he would introduce a football-related anecdote to get it back on track. Though I didn't really blame him (Motty), not blaming him made me think. You have to endeavour not to be like that when you're like me.

the car park. Did I remember to bring the car-park ticket? Did I even get one? We play 'The Boys Are Back in Town' in the car because the club play them when we come out on to the pitch, an appropriate anthem, with its faintly absurd air of braggadocio. If it wasn't the case before, it's true now that I've come to think of 'The Boys Are Back In Town' as a magnificent song. And there's a routine for the return too: the manager's apologia on Radio Stoke as we crawl away from the stadium, the phone-in on *606* which gets us all the way to Cambridge Services, a brief listen to that wanker Westwood on Radio One, and finally the second playing of the hip-hop tape as we pass out of Thetford Forest. Away matches are the same with the added novelty of getting lost while marvelling at the inanity of a station like Radio Posh instead of Radio Stoke.

It's utterly emptying to have the prospect dragged from under you.

And, to make matters worse, there we were in the middle of nowhere, in some flatland in the vague vicinity of Swaffham, not even all that far from Peterborough, and it wasn't even raining. Waterlogged pitch my arse.

Mickey-Mouse Second-Division two-bob shite, I muttered.

What's two-bob, Dad?

Which at least gave me the opportunity to explain the difference between today's entry prices and those that applied when I was his age (augmented by tales of seventies hooliganism, very popular with the boy, though failing to work their magic on this occasion) as we U-turned towards an entirely pointless afternoon back in Norwich.

Back on the road to Preston North End

Deepdale is a neat, picturesque football ground. If the three tidy, modern stands indicate the home side's ambition – not to mention their ability to protect their heritage by redeveloping on their traditional site rather than moving their stadium to a wind-blasted hill beside an incinerator – the antique shed on the fourth side is a leitmotif, as all around the money required to finish the job runs out. But the shed stands as a reminder of a different era too, and as the teams take to the field on another sunny afternoon – Preston in their famous white shirts, us in our famous stripes – the line-ups, if you narrow your eyes to fade out the sponsor logos, look for all the world a throwback to the fifties.

Stoke edge the first ten minutes. The wonderboy Commons makes a run at their defence, causing a defender to upend him. Penalty. This is more than we could have hoped for. Clarkey, our left-back – slight, callow, a bit dodgy at being a left-back, though he is at least left-footed – steps up to take it. Is Clarkey our penalty-taker now then? Top corner! *Yeesss*! But the ref orders it re-spotted. I'm at the opposite end of the ground, I can't work out the reason for this. Bastards, even when they've given us a penalty they try to prevent us from scoring. But, from the retake, Clarkey sends it home again. 1–0. C'MON. Minutes later the ref, in the way of refs, squares the situation by giving *them* a penalty. It's hit wide. Bloody hell – what can this be? To the untrained eye it looks not unlike *luck*. And Preston have already had a shot saved point-blank on the line by our keeper Cutler – God-like, handsome, suspect on crosses – and before the half is up they've hit the bar twice and missed an absolute sitter as well as wasting the penalty. They have also scored twice too. *All* in front of us. As we attempt our half-time refreshments – a chicken balti pie is challenge enough on its own without a churning stomach to go with it – we can consider ourselves lucky not to have conceded seven. Hip-hop plays out of the PA. Even though I've spotted and spoken to Graham Etherington's sister, and been talking to strangers around where I've been sitting (though no fellow Stokie is truly a stranger, and talking to people you don't know in our crowd is absolutely allowed, you are NOT a nutter for doing it), I miss Jack's company. He'd have something to say about this, the first ever recorded instance of a decent half-time MC.

Ten minutes into the second half they score another, one of their forwards waltzing through our defence and making it look much too easy. 3–1. The time has come to remember that Preston were in a play-off final, ninety minutes away from the Premiership, only two seasons back. To acknowledge that you never expect to win when you play away. To say it's not been a bad game. That our lads haven't been outclassed, even if our defending could be described as thoroughly primitive. And then we are given *another* penalty. This strikes me as double the amount we were awarded during the whole of last year. In *one* match. Unprecedented. Clarkey simply has to miss, this being his third spot-kick of the game, given the retake. He slots it home, bottom corner. 3–2. We spend the last quarter of an hour trying to assist the ball into the net by shouting. Five minutes added time are announced. In the fourth of these Commons runs at them again, scarifying the Preston defence into conceding a corner which Commons takes himself. It flies into the box and Cookie, in a diving-and-heading comic-strip-hero last-minute-of-extra-time-equalizer-type-scenario, scores and rescues a point. 3–3! The time has come to fly into the arms of your fellow man, woman or child in a deranged manner. We know this activity as 'a Mental'. Superb. By far the greatest team the world has ever seen. The ref will blow full-time immediately after the restart. It's a formality. But he doesn't. Still, from their kick-off, we win the ball back. Now we lose it, in midfield. A Preston player is running through our defence. We've tried to play offside, and failed. He *has* run through our defence. This cannot happen. The whistle must sound, the ref *must* blow. The Preston player is going to score. Please blow ref. Please. The Preston player rounds Cutler. *Now*, blow it NOW. The Preston player slots the ball behind Cutler. 4–3. The ref blows full-time.

In the coming weeks I might be able to consider that this game was a classic, a thriller, one of the best I've ever been to, and that, rather impressively, and against expectation, the match of the day actually *did* turn out to be the one I made the 500-mile round-trip to see. But several hours and several pints of anaesthetic later, the best I am able to say is that, when you equalize in the last-minute-but-one, for fuck's sake, your responsibility as a professional football player, for fuck's sake, for which you are paid a nice fat wad, is to hoof the fucking ball out of the ground until the ref blows full-time. Your responsibility as a professional football player, for which you are paid a nice fat wad, for fuck's sake, is *not* to fucking fanny about in midfield allowing the opposition to nick the ball and score a ninety-fifth fucking-minute fucking winner you fucking cnuts.

For fuck's fucking sake.

Every match is a big match for someone

It's a Bank Holiday weekend. It's given over to two fixtures. Norwich at Stoke follows the Deepdale débâcle. I'm worried (a permanent condition). The Canaries were a mere penalty shoot-out from the Premiership last season. The day after Stoke's victory at the Millennium Stadium, Norwich lost to Birmingham City in the Division One play-off. Jack and I were still in the Welsh capital on the morning of this game as Norwich and Birmingham fans began arriving in town. Prior to our victory, no team allocated the stadium's south dressing room – Birmingham's for the day – had won a final. The Birmingham fans, glancing upon Jack, who had not changed out of his replica shirt, were keen to touch him, for luck, as if he were a chimney sweep, because in winning our match we had additionally 'broken the dressing-room jinx'. Jack was only too happy to oblige. To add to his new-found guru-like charm-effect status, he calmly reassured Birmingham's fans that they would win, easy. Because, to conclude a weekend that was already going very well indeed, he needed Norwich to lose. Why? In order to see Stoke competing in the same division as them in the year ahead. Why? Because, if it isn't bad enough for him to be supporting a rubbish team from miles away, it's made worse when that team plays in a league lower than the team his mates support. This is a situation which can only bring about unrequired txt sledging:

U lost agenst Bury U 4King to$$ers :-)

Not to mention the actual verbal itself at first break on Monday and continuing throughout the rest of the school week.

The nightmare scenario for Jack (and for me, on both his and my own behalf) was that as we finally came up, Norwich would move on ahead of us. Such a turn of events would deny us vital elements in our promotion year, most importantly season-long divisional parity and the opportunity so afforded for year-round results comparisons: *We* beat Ipshit, didn't we – remind us again, what was the score when they hammered you 2–0 . . .? Also, and just as importantly, if not even more so, if that's possible, for the pair of games that we'd otherwise miss out playing against *them*. So we were more than heartily cheered that at the finish of a nailbiting encounter which ended in a penalty shoot-out, the Birmingham players proved to be immensely more talented at sticking it in the back of the net from twelve yards than the Norwich players, who were amusingly hapless at it. Unkind, uncharitable, cruel and residentially-treacherous as this may have been, the last thing we wanted to see in our glory year was Arsenal, Liverpool and all the rest glamorously turning up at Carrow Road while we drove hundreds of miles to see us lose 4–0 to Rotherham. That would be *too* much to bear.

So here was the first real fruit of the outcome of those play-off matches. And there was Jack still in Spain with his mum. How unfair was that? When he saw the fixture list, he was like: No way. And I was like: Jack, you can't expect your mum to plan your holidays around the possibility that Stoke might be promoted, that would be *insane* . . .

'But dad . . .'

'No "but Dad". And *nobody* could predict we'd meet them while you were away . . .'

'But D . . .'

'No "but D. . ."'

'But . . .'

'No "but . . ."'

'B . . .'

'No "b . . ."'

Sorry as I am, sad as I am, much as I understand, empathize, am gutted on behalf of, and feel for the lad, it is *not* in my power to get his holiday cancelled for a football match, even for one of this significance.

'. . .'

'No ". . ."'

And it has to be said that being abroad is nothing like as awkward, sports newswise, as it used to be. For the supporter caught out on holiday, there's no longer the need to wait forty-eight hours for a day-old paper. The moments spent hovering and twitching by the empty news rack, the tense wait prior to delivery, the cursory exchange with your like-minded brother hovering beside you[10] – They're usually here by twelve, must be a hold-up at the airport or summat – are over.[11]

Who can honestly say that the global-info age hasn't improved life immensely? A couple of years ago in Crete, I had occasion to make an emergency visit to an internet café to establish that we had scraped into the play-offs via the last game of the season, minutes after this had actually happened – quarter-to-seven, local time. Bliss, albeit of an arrested and autistic variety.

And now Jack was able to access information about the development of the fixture instantly, by text, from me – he'd set up his international roaming with this express purpose in mind.

The first message I sent to Spain read as follows:

0–0 H/T

It had been comfortable, as it turned out. The Canaries didn't look all they might be cracked up to be. But they opened

---

10 Always a Newcastle United supporter. I salute their devotion.

11 And when they did arrive, you'd hand over hundreds of drachma for a *Daily Mirror* only to discover that you'd lost 0–4 away to who-the-fucking-hell-are-Reading, had two sent off (this is a true story) and that there wasn't even so much as a hopelessly inadequate match report to accompany the shocking bare statistics in the results round-up. Same with the next game three days later, more hundreds of drachma: lost 0-4 to Bolton. A typical Stoke sequence.

the second half by scoring almost immediately, a consequence of our all-new thoroughly primitive style of defending. No. No. No no no no no. The thought of having to relay F/T news of a Norwich victory was too horrible to contemplate, knowing how it would ruin the remainder of his holiday. An unwelcome tension began to build in my head. This always happens when we go behind, but it was worse than usual, my internal pressure-cooker being overheated by the admixture-prospect of having to be the bearer of terrible news. But Stoke pushed forward. We were playing our best football since promotion – flowing, energetic attack. We had them well under. But we couldn't score, and as the pressure on the pitch kept building, so it did in my head, and even though we sang, singing was not enough to release it. There is only *one* thing that *can* release it, and that one thing was delivered.

Commons surged from the halfway line, played a one-two with Freezer (another junior, Marc Goodfellow, nicknamed as: 'For-he's-a' jolly Goodfellow) and lashed the return from well outside the area. The ball beat the diving keeper. It could have been going in or it could have been going wide. It hit the foot of the upright and span. From that gyroscopic condition it flirted across the line to strike the other upright where it found the necessary angle to kick backwards. I have never seen a ball take so long to fizz into the net. Behind the goal, I mentalized with my mum and Trezza and Graham Etherington – family, lover and friend – and mentally I mentalized with Jack too. My head lightened as the pressure dissipated. During the course of play, only a goal can achieve this effect, and this was a great one, so the cure was almost instant. If you don't get the goal, the tension can only fall away gradually, over the coming hours, without any sense of catharsis, though alcohol speeds the process. All the same, it's an unpleasant, unwelcome and unjoyous experience lacking any effective 'closure'. This clearly isn't an affliction from which our board suffer,[12] otherwise they'd have bought a proper striker long ago. Because Commons, fabulous though he is (new worry: forget Cardiff – hundreds of scouts from everywhere in the main stand), is not really playing in a position to score goals, he's playing in a position to supply them.

Txt: 1–1 F/T

Rtn txt: Yes yes yes!!! That's better for us than for those yellow shite Innit?! xx J

And in the spirit of my son, I find the time, while walking back across the car park, to abuse some Norwich supporters, accusing them of being jammy gits, and advising them to cart-off back to Norfolk and to go and make out with some farmyard animals. Dear oh dear. I've haven't offered that sort of recommendation to a fellow human being on a one-to-one basis since silk scarves knotted round wrists went out of

---

12 It helps them that half the time they're not there. The Icelandics tend to be up to something more interesting in Iceland. The others, of whom more later, prefer to spend their time surfing the net for personalized reg plates.

fashion. Except to traffic wardens. How to explain this atavistic return? I mean, I *live* in Norwich; I'm travelling back there myself as soon as I've dropped my mum off (who, along with Trezza, is far from impressed). What's my problem?

My problem

It's problems plural, as follows:

1) Norfolk, despite its widely received image as a backward, yokel-heavy location, is also full of conservatives with big and small c, yuppies, Hooray Henries, patricians, the landed gentry, shooting rights, second homes, country fayres, mansion houses, thoroughbred horses and a vulgar excess of sports utility vehicles. Or, to put it another way, it's full of money. Stoke-on-Trent South, on the other hand, where the Britannia is situated, is 376th on the list of wealthy constituencies in England, or to put it another way, last. Although Norwich and Stoke aren't that far separate on a line of latitude, Norwich is a part of the affluent South, whereas Stoke-on-Trent remains an unrecovered sprawling mess in the broken, de-skilled, North. (Stoke is in the Midlands, of course, but on a North/South-divide, it's in the North.) I don't like it. The financial contrast is too marked. And the cultural contrast follows on. Stoke's economy operates almost entirely in the area of knock-off. In Stoke, for example, you never see anyone smoking fags marked: 'UK Duty Paid', though you do see a lot of people smoking a lot of fags (smoking

is compulsory in the Potteries). Norwich, on the other hand, has a city centre in which shops which sell t-shirts for a hundred quid a throw can flourish. Some people might say, If you feel so strongly, why don't you clear off back and live there?

2) It's the nature of moving away that you are in some way dissatisfied with the environment of the motherlode. Freeing yourself from your region is not an unusual imperative in your late teens. This does not mean that you will not defend that region's honour to your death. My initial departure was to London, on Tebbitt's bike, in Thatcher's eighties, but I'd have gone anyway. I worked in various manual jobs, was violently homesick, but determined to ride it out. After all, what awaited me if I returned while Maggie and her posse were carrying through their project? The dole. One vital way that I kept in touch with my roots was through my team: on the radio every Saturday afternoon, plus going to matches, and therefore being with my own people for a few hours, whenever we played in the capital or thereabouts. It helped. And it helped maintain my identity. For a while I was that hardy irritant to Londoners – the Professional Northerner. (For the purposes of Londoners, the North begins on the south side of Highgate Cemetery, but anyway, what chance do you have of explaining anything to them about geography when they say, Oi mate, you talk just like like that Paul McCartney, mate. No chance whatsoever. And you don't sound nuffink like him, neither, by the way, Guv.)

A few years later, having met Marion, Jack's mum, and having Jack arrive, we decided we didn't want to stay in London. Marion is from Aberdeen. Moving there was clearly out of the question. Watch Scottish football!? I did it once and that was more than enough, thanks. There was never the remotest possibility of Jack going to the bad in the way of supporting Aberdeen either, as they are simply one of the teams who aren't Rangers or Celtic. Returning to Stoke was out of the question too. Marion was as keen on that idea as I was to go Caledonian, and, as by this time I was making a living rag-rolling walls, a job-description that would get you laughed out of the Potteries, it was a double no-no. But rag-rolling is a job-description that wouldn't entirely get you laughed out of Norwich, and for which you could even pick up reasonable money. So we ended up in East Anglia in part through earning possibilities, but equally, more significantly, through having friends in the city and through both of us liking the place.

I could have returned since this time. But I haven't.

So: I do not want to piss off back to Stoke, because, quite clearly, I want to be elsewhere. But, as the renowned French psychoanalyst Jacques Lacan has it (making the logical extension to the Cartesian, I think, therefore I am): I think where I am not, therefore I am not where I think. In other words, wherever my physical body might be, my mind is often in Stoke. Or in other, other words, You can take the boy out of the gutter . . .

3) There is worse to come. You might like to think of yourself as a working-class hero, but by becoming a writer you have crossed the great divide; you are standing about at a literary party in London and you notice that the fear and the loathing is everywhere in the air, especially the loathing. The

backhanded compliment is the order *de nos jour*. Congratulations: you have made it to the middle classes. In this light, it's not such a surprise that Norwich is the place where you have found yourself. In addition to being moneyed, it is also vastly overpopulated with poets, Hare Krishnas, shiatzuists, colonic-irrigators, crystalists, importers of Javan furniture, healing craft centres and the like. For fuck's sake. But. All this notwithstanding, I *still* like the place: historic buildings are not knocked down to make way for a new TescoShiteStore; it's not seen as poncey to talk about art and culture, etc. I like art and culture, etc; I used to be a rag-roller. In Norwich there are bars where you can find a selection of decent glasses of wine. When I took Trezza to a pub in Stoke's shopping centre and she asked for a dry white, she was offered Liebfraümilch. When she declined, the barmaid thought for a second before suggesting, We've got cider – that's dry. While this may be comical, it's also retarded. So who am I to be having anything to say about yokels? As a consequence of all this:

4) I am a divided soul, torn between where I come from and where I am; between what I was and what I've become. But:

5) I know which side I'm on. And:

6) There is no arena in which I feel as clearly my sense of the side I'm on as when I'm one of the crowd that follows Stoke City. Normally, in any other circumstance, I don't even like crowds. But in this one I feel at home. The more matches I go to – and here, I suppose, is the point – the more often I go home.

*

Perhaps all this explains what might be going on when I find myself abusing strangers with whom I share a city about mythic acts of sheepshagging. Oh, and incidentally, just in case it seems that there is a solution which might help in the unification of my self, not to mention save vast amounts on petrol, oil, snacks and motor-depreciation:

7) I could never support a team that plays in yellow. It is a colour that totally fails to stir the football in my soul.

7a) I could never support any other team at all. Full stop.

A necessary word about our box-office personnel

The game that follows the magnificent scoring draw against the sheepshaggers of Norwich takes place a few miles along the A50 from Stoke against the sheepshaggers of Derby. They call us Clayheads. Because of the pottery businesses. They should be able to come up with a better insult than one that needs an explanation. This match attracts restrictions to the effect that Stoke fans may travel by *club coach only*, provided they are a season ticket holder or a member. That's what it said in the programme. On the official club website (*Pravda*) it says actually *last* year's membership will suffice. Being early season, last year's membership is all I've got at the moment. I must sort this out, though I like there to be an element of danger in the procurement of tickets. This is one reason why I'm not a season ticket holder. The other reason is that once you've got your season ticket you're stuck in the same pocket of fans, and even if you're not sat next to Mr Bean, a strong-but-silent type, a signed-on fascist, or a maniac of other description for the whole year, there'll be one near enough by to drive you insane. If you purchase tickets on a match-by-match basis you at least spread your risk on that front. And as we are nowhere near selling out, ticket-procurement is not really all that risky a procedure. It's not like at Arsenal, for example, where they have a seven-year waiting list just for *membership*.

Anyway, the website information being at odds with the programme information, I pick up the phone. To be honest though, you can't be sure that a phone call will clarify matters.

A typical conversation with someone from the ticket office:

ME: Hello, I'd like two tickets for the game versus Port Fail, please.

TICKET OFFICE WORKER: It's an all-ticket match, that.

ME: I know, that's why I want tickets – I'm a member, by the way.

T/O WORKER: A member of what?

ME: Of the club, I've got a membership card, you know, it's red and white plastic, like a credit card.

T/O WORKER: What's it say on it?

ME: It says Potters Club.

T/O WORKER (*aside, to co-worker, but not what you'd call* sotto voce): Says he's a member.

CO-WORKER: A member of what?

T/O WORKER (*aside, to co-worker*): Potters Club.

CO-WORKER (*aside back to main worker*): Not Legends?

T/O WORKER: Is it Legends you're a member of, duck?

ME: No. Potters Club.

T/O WORKER (*aside, to co-worker*): No, he *still* says Potters Club.

Muffled sounds, possible disconnection.

ME: Hello . . . hello . . .

T/O WORKER: Right, duck, Potters Club you say . . . how many tickets is it you're after?

ME: Two.

T/O WORKER: All right then, I can do you two for . . . (*quotes a figure which varies each and every time*)

ME: Thanks, that's excellent.

T/O WORKER: Will you be coming in to pick them up or shall I put them in the post?

Though I have little-to-no faith in the following stage of the transaction being successful, I am *not* going to drive over from Norwich for them, am I? And this introduces an extra-extra element of risk to keep the gambler in me happy: the mail and the chance of finding items in amongst the bills and the junk that I actually want. Or not.

On match days, there are signs over the ticketing office windows reading Tickets for Todays (sic) Match Only. They're the kind of windows that have a slot at the bottom like you get in banks. Depending on which one you approach, many other transactions can be conducted through those slots. In reality you *can* buy tickets for many other games aside from Todays, as well as lottery tickets, bingo and Lotto tickets, concert tickets, vouchers and coupons for things you don't understand, all sorts. Behind that glazing they operate on the old Eastern-bloc model: once you're a worker in the system you're effectively self-employed. It's an attitude I admire, it appeals to the freelancer in me (the character who's always urging the gambler to strike bets). One can only imagine what might be on offer to members of Legends.

Unsurprisingly, their modus operandi meant that I spoke to them many many times in respect of acquiring tickets to see this game versus Derby County with the attached restrictions.

They smelt of pubs and Wormwood Scrubs and too many right-wing meetings

If you were supporting Stoke and didn't travel to the game on a *club coach only* and were found anywhere near the ground, before kick-off, you would be arrested. Matters of civil liberties are at issue here, clearly, and our supporters were severely taken aback to be the subject of a police escort for the whole of the sixty-odd-mile round journey from Stoke. On arrival in Derby they were denied access to any area of the town whatsoever with the exception of the the heavily policed tarmac leading to the turnstiles which give entrance to Pride Park and the few square metres of the away end itself. They were far from amused. For me, all matches are difficult to get to. I was less pissed-off than the majority because I didn't have to take part in exactly the same pantomime as the majority. We exiles had our own slightly different pantomime.

Why was it like this?

This is the situation: *we* have some Prominents and *they* have some Prominents. Prominent is the police-vogue word for hooligan.

The police decided that these measures were in the best interests of the structural integrity of the buildings of Derby, not to mention the personal safety of the citizens of Derby and anybody else who happened to be passing through. It was heavy-handed, temper-inducing, inflammatory; the Prominents would meet up anyway in a well-planned rendezvous later on, but there you had it. It was a 12.00 kick-off to avoid drink-related behaviour. Our police still live in some sort of Dixon of Dock Greenland where the pubs don't open until lunchtime and people don't start drinking until midday.

All this meant *we* left Norwich at about six in the morning to join an even more exclusive coach than the rest, the Exiles' Special. The meeting point was a service station on the A50, near Derby itself. This location was selected in order to avoid the situation of Stoke supporters who live in Derby having to drive from Derby to Stoke to get on the bus, and there and back again after the match to collect their cars and return home. To Derby. Where they would presumably be placed on file and suffer harassment and persecution for the rest of their unfortunate Stoke-supporting lives.

After the many phone calls to our ticket office, we had secured our tickets for the Exiles' Special.

In between these exchanges I had cause to call the Derbyshire Constabulary Football Liaison Officer, to enquire about these arrangements. During the conversation, it occurred to me that we could be ambushed at the service station by the Derby Prominents, who go under the name of the DLF (Derby Lunatic Fringe), a thought I put to the Liaison Officer.

Do you wear a shirt? she asked.

She meant football colours by this. Not wishing to say anything that might later be used in evidence against me I admitted only that it wasn't out of the question that I might have a scarf round my neck.[13]

They won't be after you then, they have their own clothes, you know, that designer stuff, Burberry, they're only interested in fighting with each other, she said. They arrange it all by mobile.

I knew about the clothes and about the off-terrace rumbles. Everybody does. The cellphone communication, though obvious after less than a second's thought, somehow came to me as a new idea.

They have the mobile numbers of the, er, Prominents from other clubs you mean? Of each other? I said.

That's right, the Liaison Officer replied.

---

13 Prominents refer to non-hooligans as Scarfers.

A magnificent scene crossed my mind –

PROMINENT 1 (*speed dials*): Here, d'you fancy gettin your
    head smashed in?
PROMINENT 2: That'd be bloomin marvellous. Name your
    weapons.
PROMINENT 1: I thought Smirnoff Ice bottles would be
    nice.
PROMINENT 2: You're on. My place or yours?

A conversation developed about what, therefore, was the point
in making the match all-ticket and imposing farcical travel
arrangements on the good old majority of innocent supporters,
when in fact, the hoolis, as we affectionately know them, would
be arranging to smash up a pub *somewhere* later in the day in
any event, either in Derby or possibly in an entirely different
location where a match was, or wasn't, taking place –
Wolverhampton, for example, or maybe Macclesfield, wherever
they thought it best. It was a circular conversation, as you might
expect, about damage limitation, which the Liaison Officer
repeatedly punctuated with the bemused phrases that she
'didn't know what sort of mentality these people had' and that
she 'couldn't understand them'.

From close observation, I can say that they have the
mentality of a person who adores a scrap and likes to wear the
same clothes as his mates. Sounds familiar from somewhere.
Ours are called the Naughty 40 (really), amongst the chic-er
element of our crowd (context is all here), sharp, though

pissed-up, and not without a certain black wit. I noticed one at Derby who'd replaced his Stone Island tag – the other crucial designer label – with a button-on badge: Football Supporters Against Violence. Down to their unlikely names – to be threatened by the Derby Lunatic Fringe strikes me as akin to being terrorized by the Tooting Popular Front (though it will undoubtedly feel different if you catch yourself in the wrong place at the wrong time and find one of them coming at you with an attitude problem and the Smirnoff Ice) – they're a sort of throwback to the first mod era, Faces. It would be nice to think that in their appropriation of the Burberry Check they operate a deeply ironic sartorial code. The red, camel, black and white country cloth designed at the turn of last century as 'outdoor wear for sportsmen' is a perfect choice of outfit for an activity that is entirely about hunting in packs. But actually, I'm afraid they're just copying Mrs David Beckham's taste in schmutter. Our hooligans, the N40, are the most successful in the country. The one league we top. Why?

Are we instinctively good at fighting in Stoke? *You're going home in a fucking ambulance* was one of our welcoming calls to opposition fans when I was a teenager, and was not a wholly idle boast. So, yes, we are pretty good at it. But we're also the most poverty-stricken city in the country and that has to translate into something tangible. Some of our young men might reasonably feel that they've got nothing to lose. So: why not rob some designer gear, travel to other depressed post-industrial areas and chant lyrics like *You're just a town full of*

Pakis at the home support? You know it makes sense. It's got to make you feel better.

On first hearing this song, Jack thinks the word 'Pakis' is 'Pikeys', the common slang for gypsies or travellers (with the modish added-on meaning signifying an absence of quality: Poundland, for example is a 'Pikey shop').

Town full of Pikeys? Dad, what are they on about?

In his mishearing he brings something of his day-to-day experience. The Asian population in Norfolk is barely visible. Racism exists, in rural areas in particular, in a peculiarly archaic form whereby it wouldn't be out of the question to hear an old person making a request to touch a black child for luck, like fingering a chimney sweep, or being crossed by a black cat. Out here on the Eastside, then, it's the gyppos, inbreds and Pikeys who attract the prejudice. And at its margins, when not denoting low specification consumer items, Pikey has the loosest of definitions: it's a casual playground term of abuse for anyone you don't like.

Jack is dumbfounded when the chant gets its second outing (it's not sung by many, but neither is it shouted down) when he has to agree that it *is* Pakis that they're singing. Because Jack is black, in the way that Ali-G is black. It is not right to dis his brothers in this way. Boyakasha.

It turns out to be a busy time for the downside of football life. This was his second dose of racism of the week. We'd been down to West Ham for a night match.

How to deal with this shit?

The best part of the Derby experience, as it turned out, *was* travelling by club coach only on the Exiles' Special.

In air-conditioned, police-escorted comfort we rolled along the hard shoulder of the dual-carriageway and were waved through red lights on a seamless journey to the ground. There we were greeted by the PCs, ranked in double-lane formation, as far as the eye could see, and filmed as we approached the entrances: the faces of our Faces are certainly known, they're captured by police video at many of the grounds we visit, not to mention regularly at our own place.[14] The Exiles' Special coach enjoyed the added kudos of being the sole bus not leaving from Stoke, and we appreciated having our own dedicated outriders, motorbike to the front, Range Rover to the rear. Deluxe. An almost impossible condition of travel to achieve without being royalty, villain, or follower of the Rip-Roaring Mighty Potters. We were a quiet wrecking crew, consisting mostly of middle-aged and older people and children.

Once inside the stadium, though, there were only about a third as many of us as might be expected because the other two-thirds who should have been there couldn't be fucked with this

---

14 Our fans go in for nice rococo Punch and Judy routines as riot-equipped coppers play their zoom lenses over the crowd.

carry-on. Not to mention that such arrangements come at a price. My ticket for this was £31. Usually it'd be about £15–£20. And, economic considerations aside, most people simply aren't stupid enough to put up with being treated like Her Majesty or a serial murderer just to watch a crap football match. We were wank, shipping two late goals after being outplayed by a pedestrian Derby team. We never ever looked anything like scoring.

This was Jack's first game on his return from Spain. Driving back to Norwich, I felt I had to give him an option on a get-out clause. I asked him how much longer he thought he could put up with it, advising him he didn't have to keep doing it for me, emphasising that I really meant it, that he really didn't, and that I was sure he could find better ways of spending his Saturdays like staying in bed til the afternoon then taking a leisurely cruise round his project in the company of his massive and checking out the hoes. His response, after the snort he does to denote that I am not funny even if I think I am, was to pick up the newspaper from the floorwell, to examine the sport pages, specifically the tables.

Dad, what's the nearest Premiership club to where I was born?

Charlton Athletic.

I glanced sideways, I could see where his mind was going. He had already begun examining himself for having Arsenal as his top-tier side, he was starting to think it made him too much of a glory-hunting twat. In addition to this, Arsenal-supporting was beginning to cause him an identifiable extra problem: it was raising his expectations too high in terms of following Stoke.

You can't support Charlton though, can you? I said. (They're boring, crap, anti-glamour, and play in horrible shirts.)

No, he said. They're boring, crap, anti-glamour, and play in horrible shirts, he said.

The next nearest two are Chelsea and West Ham. Neither is all that local to his Lambeth birthplace, though Arsenal, as I pointed out, is even further away. It took no time at all for us to acknowledge that he couldn't transfer to Chelsea, since they're just a loose collective of overseas mercenaries with no heart or soul, not actually a team, as understood in the old sense. You might as well follow Nike. But West Ham are a different story. Like most clubs they're fairly hopeless and therefore easier to identify with. Joe Cole was Jack's favourite England player (*and* – then – a local hero and *not* a well-travelled mercenary); Paolo Di Canio, scorer of sublime goals, is many a fan's favourite-player-from-another-club, and England left-winger Trevor Sinclair (Jack's own position) and goalkeeper David James are as cool and charismatic as footballers come: you just know they drive away from matches with hip-hop rattling the body panels of their SUVs. Like Jack, Sinclair and James is black, but unlike Jack they is actually black as well innit. As a final selling point, claret and blue shirts, we were able to agree, are a decent strip. As it happened, West Ham were playing Charlton that afternoon, a game we kept more than a weather ear on as we returned from our early kick-off, as the commentaries switched around the country.

West Ham lost 2–0, a result which left them bottom of the League.

That's the team for me, said Jack.

I could do nothing but admire his pragmatic approach to easing the problem of StokeLife. Well, I *could* do one thing.

Shall I see if I can get tickets for a game at Upton Park then?

As we have yet to discover a saturation point for watching live football, this was not a difficult question for him to answer. Admission to Premiership grounds, if you are not a member of the club in question, comes at a premium. However, as luck would have it, we were able to purchase a pair for a game taking place just a few days after this new allegiance was struck, at half-price, because they were playing against newly-promoted West Brom who were considered not much of an attraction. Who would argue with that?

It was a midweek in East London, it was a

Night match

Floodlight breaking through the darkness transforms the most mundane location – the low industrial estate around Colchester's Layer Road ground, for example – into an arena full of promise and expectation.

Away night matches are superb, giving a schoolboy something to look forward to all day, getting him through double-maths, skipping him off the last period for a phony dental appointment and offering the possibility of missing double-chemistry first thing tomorrow too, following a post-midnight return/sleeping-in-in-the-morning type situation (post-recovery from oral trauma, ooh dear my gum do hurt.).

As winter approaches and more evening fixtures are announced as rescheduled games and cup-ties and replays fill the blanks in the calender, is it too fanciful to believe that the ritual journey to the illuminating of the sky in some part satisfies the primitive human craving for which fire-worship used to provide?

How to deal with *this* shit?

As West Ham kicked off under the lights and put on a display of skilled, fluid, penetrating football in this exotic (for us) new location (Plaistow) I could see Jack thinking, Wow, this is an entirely different game to the one Stoke play. It was certainly what I was thinking, and I worried that he might be completely seduced. The full house with the two-and-a-half-times-bigger crowd than ours, only added to the effect. West Brom looked unremarkable in comparison to the Hammers, but they scored from their only attempt at goal, and after that West Ham faded as their supporters got on the team's back – their singing was nowhere near as good as Stoke's, but their bleating was up there with the best. Are they Norwich in disguise? They lost by the single goal.

What did you make of that then? I asked as we shuffled towards the exit.

Just like Stoke, only worse, because they're better, he replied, pulling his mushroom face as we made our way round the edge of the stadium.

And . . .?

Oh, they're the team for me, he said. They're the Stoke of the Prem all right.

We edged away with the crowd, passing by the stopped buses, the purveyors of hamburgers and hot dogs, the mounted police, the dogs, the vendors of shirts and insignia. Above our heads children in saris hung out of the windows of the flats above the shops on Green Street, entertaining themselves by observing the sights and sounds of the dispersing crowd. We drove away through streets narrowed by jammed and double-parked cars, passing the Plaistow Park Community Centre, where, at 10.15 on a Wednesday week night, an Asian bride and groom emerged to the home-video camera, their expressions cast as if they were enduring a shotgun affair. Maybe they had simply heard the score. We were hemmed tight enough to have to fold in the wing mirrors, as from the opposite direction a Volkswagen driven by a member of So Solid Crew – a starring hip-hop outfit on the pre-match tapes – squeezed by. Slunk low in the passenger seat, in a post-defeat gloom, Jack was nonetheless taking it all in.

Did you hear that racism back there? he said.

No, I replied.

C'mon, you must've.

No. What did they say?

He says that some man behind him said that Kanoute was a useless black bastard.

Frederic Kanoute? Really? I said. Yeah, *really*, he replied. (You can be massively dense sometimes, can't you, Dad.)

Saying that about one of their own players, he said, That's bad though. Innit?

Wouldn't it be just as bad if it were said about a West Brom player?

Yeah, but it's even worse when it's your own player. It's not good support, is it?

No.

As the traffic loosened and we headed out through Essex, up the M11, and he fell asleep, I thought about the casual racism that I didn't even hear. Do I blank it out, is that what happens now; after years of going to football, have I become totally inured to it, does it just pass me by as part of the scenery? Even at Norwich City, which prides itself on being a 'family club' it's not unusual to hear some mutant referring to an athlete in full flight as a bloody black something or another.

Actually, I do notice that, but they're not my crowd. It's not my business.

On the Saturday after West Ham, our third match of the week, hundreds of miles away to the north, at Burnley, we found ourselves on the edge of our Prominents, because at half-time we'd moved seats to be closer to the pitch. It was now that Jack became sure that it *was* Paki, not Pikey, being chanted because in the row behind us grown men were unmistakably bellowing, *You're just a town full of Pakis*. This is my crowd. This is my business.

Did I turn round and tell this pondlife to shut the fuck up? No. Why not? Because, aside from the scene that this would involve – that is, aside from my own personal cowardice – I'm not going to change a tadpole's mind about anything. The tadpole's mind is made up, and I'm tempted to the belief that it can no more not be a racist tadpole than I cannot support Stoke. For the tadpole, racism is a lifelong affiliation. For me, it's my lifelong affiliation to my club that is the reason why I don't remove myself from the company of this frogspawn, as I would in any other situation.

On Saturdays in the mid-eighties when I was that angry young man operating one of several of my post-Waddington Stoke City boycotts I would have been as likely to be found at a Rock Against Racism or Anti-Apartheid rally as anywhere else. Apartheid's gone, but not because I marched, because economic circumstances laid it low. South Africa hasn't eliminated its racists, and neither have we. I've given up believing that rocking or marching or hip-hopping against the bomb can eradicate racism or anything else. It might make it less generally acceptable, but does it actually effect a change? Can lifelong affiliations *be* eradicated? It might be that I've given up on the possibility of changing congenital attitudes, and that all I'm left to conclude is that the only thing we have the ability to do (I'm talking here of, and as an example of, a white English male) is to carry on with something and to let the other bastards carry on with their stuff too. How many times do you see some germ drop litter in the street and do nothing about it? The answer, in my case, is too often. Because you know for certain the germ will continue its litter-dropping whatever you say. That's the best I can come up with, for explaining how I deal with this shit. To say I know it to be unstoppable. Actually, maddened enough once or twice, and at a safe enough distance, I have yelled at them to shut the fuck up. It makes them louder. As for Jack, I can mark it down as part of his education to see how ignorance and intolerance is everywhere directed at people of his race, and help him to deal with it.

If I believe in anything now,

If I've one faith remaining, I believe in the upbeat of football. Are you ready for love and so on.

There was a conversation I used to have with friends where we'd argue the merits of different forms of entertainment, with the participants having to make a choice: if you were limited to watching only one type ever again, which would it be? There was a time when I'd consider their arguments that certain examples of concert, film, theatre, ballet, opera, dance or spectator sport other than football had any serious claim over watching football. (I'm not sure I gave other spectator sports any consideration, actually: *Grand Prix*? Do one, geek boy.)

I would advocate the beautiful game on the grounds that however dreary, one-dimensional, uncompelling and hackneyed the plot, all the same the moment of epiphany – the goal – was nevertheless totally plausible and transformative in every case, which is not something you can say about either *Coronation Street* or Shakespeare. I did not put it in reasoned terms like these, I merely said (possibly drunkenly, possibly repeatedly) that every game was different and that you never knew how it would end in the end.

So you'd choose a wet Wednesday watching Halifax Town playing Scunthorpe over *Carmen*, then, would you?

Carmen is a babe, and an attractive handler of a cigarette too, but all the same. Cmon, you can give me a harder one than that.

A wet Wednesday watching Halifax Town playing Scunthorpe OR Gwen Guthrie performing live at your local.

That *is* more awkward. It'd have to be Halifax Town playing Stoke.

It's become my belief that I was advocating Stoke (football) because I'm possessed by football (Stoke), because Stokefootball *owns* me in the same way that language owns me. During a seminar in a small dark room, when I returned to education in my thirties, I was knocked out of my stride as the tutor introduced the theory that language is a sign-system into which human beings enter, indeed have no choice but to enter, when they start to speak (we're not really allowed *not* to speak, are we?) – and that words have no meaning outside their role as signifiers. In the example used, a tree is only a tree because we all agree it is. Had the vocabulary developed differently, a tree might as easily be called a biscuit. Without such agreement, the word 'tree' has no latent meaning. Try saying it over and over again: see how quickly it loses its sense. In short, language has no inherent significance, words are simply a code with which we all collude. Moreover, language was here before I was here, and it'll be here long after I'm long gone – it's simply a holding tool, a system of entry, or a trap, if you like, for regulating me (or you) during my (or your) lifetime.

I found something horribly unpleasant, a feeling like déjà-vu, in this suggestion. Prior to the seminar I thought *I* was in control of the language *I* used. But I didn't invent it, did I? And I can only use it in the one way – the given way – can't I? What sort of control is that? I've come to accept that I don't have authority here, in the way I used to imagine I had, and I've come to believe a similar system is at play regarding, specifically, Stoke City, and, more widely, football. Football is simply a governing system which preceded and will post-date my life; I don't control my football habits, they control me. When Jack was a tiny boy our every weekend walk, shoulder-ride and tricycle adventure seemed magically to end up in a park where we could 1) kick a ball about, and 2) watch an amateur match while we were at it. What are the chances that *all* of our walks took us on such routes accidentally? I live in a house a two-and-a-half-minute stroll away from Carrow Road. Can this simply be chance? In an echo of my silent Sunday circuits of the old Victoria Ground, it's my habit to walk the dog round the quiet, deserted stadium late at night.

The aforementioned Jacques Lacan describes a condition he calls the Realm of the Real, which involves silence, *freedom* from the language-trap. We revert to the Realm of the Real (to pre-language, to babyness) when we are in a circumstance where speech no longer has any power, where words will not suffice, where there is nothing to say, for instance at a life's end. We often commemorate a notable death prior to a football match with a minute's silence. The silence represents a respect, but in a sense, it also represents a freedom, freedom from the mortal coil. To extend Lacan's theory, it's possible to suggest that in this shared collective silence we are able to imagine a shared collective freedom. There are moments in football stadia when a hush falls of its own accord. Graham Etherington was at the Greece–England World Cup qualifier, the occasion of David Beckham's famous last-minute free-kick goal. He tells me it was so quiet that you could actually hear the ball hit the net. There are these moments in football when we can find ourselves unexpectedly still and silent and free. It could be that it is this, this instant of freedom, which represents the true nature of the addiction (even the racists shut up). That the prospect we carry along on our journey to the game is the prospect of freedom. Then all hell breaks loose as we celebrate verbally – firstly though the intermediate semi-free inarticulate noise – *Aarrgghhhhhyyyyyeeeeeessssssssss* – and all too soon we are speaking normally – *Did you fucking see that!!!* – and once more we are back in the trap.

Football and words, these are the things I believe in. I know them both to be controlling, and I accept that that's the way it is.

International duty

But the snare does have its compensations. The idea that
football communicates across spoken barriers, for instance, is
unmistakably true:

In the early eighties,[15] as a super-enhanced part of my
boycott, I hitched through Europe with a mate. In kickabouts
in piazzas throughout the length of Italy, a country which had
just won the World Cup, and whose people were consequently
in exuberant spirits, me and the mate were skinned,

---

15 Other people associate this period with Duran Duran or Lady Di or the Mini Metro
(they may all be the same thing). I associate it with the horrendous percentage
football we played under manager Alan Durban. In *Fever Pitch* Nick Hornby relates
a quote from a press conference given by Durban following a match at Highbury.
Arsenal, in a dire game, had finally broken through our totally unambitious formation
to beat us 2–0. Durban, defending the (anti)style of football his team had employed,
snapped at the press: 'If you want entertainment, go and watch clowns.' It became
a widely reported remark, proof positive that the Corinthian spirit had died, that
results were all that mattered anymore. Hornby considers this and comes to the
conclusion that Durban was right, that it was not his job to provide entertainment,
that it was his job to look after our fans, which meant having our (poor) team avoid
defeat away from home, and that by extension Stoke supporters would be happy
with the 0–0 draw that we so clearly went looking for.

All well and good. Except: the fatal flaw – we lost 2–0 didn't we?

Durban was the third hopeless manager with club connections who is mentioned
at the beginning of this book, the last throw of the human die in the failed attempt
to avoid relegation the last time it was a probability. He was a sort of Red Adair
without the Red. Or the Adair.

nutmegged and given the right runaround by any number of scrawny Azzurri boys with the word Rossi (their hat-trick hero) felt-penned across the front of their T-shirts. This was at table football, in cappuccino bars. It was much worse out on the actual pitch (dirt car park). These skinnings and nutmeggings, though, represented friendship-points with contemporaries with whom we could not communicate verbally at all: I'm from *Stoke*, I barely speak *English* – that's how far out of the question speaking Italian would be. But through football we were invited into homes to break bread with *la famiglia*. I found this extraordinary. We were unclean for a start, like most hitchers; the only washes we were getting were when we stood out in the rain. Though Italians were unusually well-disposed towards the English at that time, on account of the war that was taking place in the south Atlantic v the Argies (on the principle, My enemy's enemy is my friend), I don't think that even speaking fluently in the host language would have allowed for such a welcome without Forza Calcio backing it up.

It's notable that one of the very first things the 'Western Alliance' did after it had bombed Afghanistan's remaining bits to even smaller bits was to try and get the Afghani national football team up and running again. Even politicians are able to understand that football is a language which allows for complex exchanges, and that a football stadium is an arena that can foster healing as equally as it can afford the opportunity for fundamentalist lunatics to flog and de-limb their fellow citizens, or for tadpoles to chant racist insults.

And so it is that, sat a row in front of those fine examples of multicultural tolerance at Burnley, when winger Bjarni Gudjonsson (*Team full of cod boys, we're just a team full of Arctic Rolls*) makes impeccable contact with an in-flight ball inside the eighteen-yard box, I find myself cheering with and for the same thing as them.

A goal.

Bjarni

He came as part of a family package with Mr G, hence his surname – Gudjonsson, son of Gudjon. Remote, difficult to read, short, prone to carrying weight, Bjarni was last season's whipping boy, accused of being a fat bastard by guys who are built along the lines of a Mr Whippy. Every club has one, a player who's singled out for abuse whenever the going gets crap. Bjarni's circumstances were exacerbated by finding himself in a sins-of-the-father type bind, though it has to be acknowledged that he had only himself to blame for the many valuable minutes of many important matches that he spent grouching out on the right wing in a cloud of ennui without any clear purpose in life. Even if such an attitude-problem was part of an ongoing family dispute, there is no excuse. When you're out there on the pitch, your responsibility is to be a boy what does good and to give 110 per cent for the team and no less.

It would have been unsurprising to see Bjarni follow Gudjon

away – he must have been upset at the duplicitous deal his dad was dealt by his erstwhile colleagues in the consortium of twats, not to mention his own treatment from the fans.

But on the other hand, who'd buy him?

Fortunately, no one. Fortunately for us, I mean, because he could never maintain his moods for entire matches, and usually made some incursive effort despite himself. He can actually dribble the ball past an opponent, which is rarer than you'd think in professional football, and is a magnificent sight to witness. Sometimes, after the dribble, he can deliver a perfect cross. And on occasion he can go on to score. I was very glad to see him stay, because at his best, when not laid low by an existential crisis, he's one of the finer talents we've seen in a Stoke shirt. He hit the greatest of strikes at dismal Layer Road one expectant floodlit night last season, teeing himself up from thirty-five yards for a shot that hammered the top corner of the net directly in front of where we stood. It was a miracle, provoked an awag (highly specialized Second-Division lunacy[16]) of a mental, and was a moment of the kind that inspired Jack to have the word Bjarni and the number '7' printed on one of the replica shirts.

The goal at Burnley was volleyed from an angle within the box to put us 1–0 in front. Volleyed goals are an example of football's capacity for the exalted: a ball taken in flight and

---

16 I was particularly taken by Manchester City's fans' response to their period in this division. They took to singing a surreal song that went: *Not really here, we're not really here . . .* An admirable coping strategy.

guided with pace and accuracy past a goalkeeper who trains all his life to prevent such an outcome requires not only an advanced level of skill but also an intuitive grasp of abstract geometry. Bjarni celebrated in his distinctive manner, with dignity, with one low bow to fans and tormenters alike in the stand behind the net. Following his father's departure, he was a player reborn. Cotterill, after trying and failing to get rid of him, dropped him for the first few games. This episode had the desirable effect of making him realize the truth of his life: that his calling is to spend his Saturday afternoons playing football for the entirety of the match. This was something he'd never had to consider under his old man, who, in the manner of many a park-team coach, always gave his boy a full game no matter how he was playing. Bjarni was quick enough to work out that to achieve his truth without nepotism meant that he had to stay interested for *the whole of the time*. He worked himself back into the starting XI, appeared to have benefitted from time spent in the gym, and began playing at a new peak. I overheard a couple of supporters leaving the stadium a few weeks later, after his fourth outstanding game in a row, expressing the thought a lot of us were having:

In top shape, looking good, playing one blinder after another: whatever must Gudjon think of him? Absolute shite week-in week-out when *he* was manager, man of the match every game now he's gone. What sort of a bloody son is *that*, eh?

Well, maybe it's the sort of son who'd found himself freed from the paternal eye, the sort of son who no longer had to worry about what his display looked like from one very specific point of view.

Aside from his talent, and his sulkily enigmatic charisma, there's one other important fact about Bjarni. He has a perfect Christian name insofar as terrace chanting of the affirmatory type goes: it's pronounced 'Byar-neey', two syllables, ending on the sympathetic *ee* sound to which footballer's names are converted as a matter of routine (Cooke–Cookie, Clarke–Clarkey, Sergei–Sergy). Though you do overhear fans having trouble with it on a one-by-one basis – Barney, Bernie – following a goal like the sublime volley, the correct enunciation is trouble-free and is sung as follows:

Byar-neey!
Byar-neey!!
Byar-neey!!!

Congratulations and celebrations

Byar-neey's personal hosannah would traditionally be followed by a burst of 'Delilah', but we barely had time to get it going at Burnley because they equalized within a minute. It all happened late on, and by the time we'd conceded *another* goal and had debut loan-signing striker Tommy Mooney sent off (Moon-eey! I think not: arrogant, temporary and very wide of the mark, if he even knows where the mark is) *our* Prominents were doing battle with *their* Prominents. The ground was heavily under-policed, because these days the clubs only pay for officers within the stadium, so they have as few inside as they can get away with. There were about twenty at Turf Moor. There were over 200 extra outside, more like the number the local force thought was really required for the fixture. In this way Burnley Football Club paid about £5,000 for policing while Lancashire Constabulary had to cover £50,000. It wasn't difficult for the Burberry brigades on either side to weigh up the odds. Goading each other all afternoon, us in the end stand, them in the stand to our side, their lot spilled on to the perimeter track at the affront of Bjarni's strike, and that was the final provocation ours needed. Small-scale skirmishing, with pockets of escalation as the Burnley team scored their goals, followed over the next few minutes. The police weren't only woefully short in numbers, they also appeared to be well under-tooled; I watched a PC attempt to fight back one of our heroes using the flexible aerial of his walkie-talkie. It's all context – the quality of the fighting was rubbish, I would've been appalled to see a truncheon used – at this I had to laugh.

It was Jack's first close-up of football Prominentism. I removed us a few rows back, but still near enough to be more or less ringside. It used to happen at nearly every game when I was his age, and on a much bigger scale; it's the sideshow that's always been on offer. Away supporters in the seventies used to attempt to 'take the home end' by surreptitiously infiltrating the terrace behind our goal prior to kick-off and waiting until about ten minutes into the match before declaring their colours. It was like a battle scene from *Spartacus* until half-time.

At the lame imitation laid on here I thought we were safe where we were. But Jack was still a bit close for his liking, and he pulled us back a few more rows. So we took up new new seats as the clock ticked down, next to an older woman supporter who was shaking her head at it all.

It's shocking, isn't it? she said.

Yes, I replied.

We just can't hold a lead can we? she said.

From 1–0 up to 2–1 down in the final quarter, a result which put us into the bottom three, into the relegation slots, for the first time. I'd stopped worrying about Cotterill playing a defensive game. In fact I wondered if it wasn't about time he considered addressing our inability to keep a clean sheet. Would extra training be out of the question? They earn enough, these fuckers, don't they? On top of everything else, the ref had been especially incompetent. And fat. I surprised myself by how enthusiastically and comprehensively I shouted atrocious words at him as he left the pitch. It's an odd arrangement at Burnley, the tunnel is in the away end, which affords a uniquely localized abuse-shouting opportunity for the away supporters as the officials take their leave. I took some low solace in observing the expression that spread across the ref's fat face – discomfort-verging-on-fear – as the fat fucker ran through us as fast as he could (not very).

It's unlike me to be like that. It's like me to have the thoughts, but to restrict myself to enjoying listening to other people voice them for me. To do my own atrocious foul-mouthed-torrenting is out of character and I put my conduct down to my proximity to the fighting moments earlier. To say I wasn't energized by it, that I hadn't received some sort of vicarious rush, would be a lie. To say that I don't enjoy our reputation for being a hard firm not to be messed with would also be a lie. In this way I can relish a certain reputation for myself even though the fact of the matter is that I'm no fighter and could accurately be described as something of a pussy.

Another reason why I am never happy at Norwich City, even as a neutral, is due to the sanitized nature of their following, too many of whom are little more than *spectators*. Norwich are one of those clubs where a PA man plays a record to prompt goal celebrations. While I don't actually require a crowd to perpetrate violence on others in order to regard them as a proper set of followers, I do at least expect them to have the wit to come up with a song of their own for when they score.

Mid-table mediocrity

For most normal supporters it's a worst-case scenario. An urgent battle against relegation gives us a reason to live every bit as much as a push for promotion. In the sequence that followed the Burnley game we won two and drew three (to set up a five-match unbeaten run!) They were all clenched-buttock affairs – we had to come from behind to draw, we had to be levelled before we could win. But: we were picking up points and heading for no-man's land. We beat Ipswich, who were supposed to be a lot better than us. This was nice for Jack back at our Eastside base, taking all three points off Norwich City's local *and* promotion rivals. That showed them. Except that, in circling away to celebrate setting up the winning goal, the wonderboy Commons damaged his cruciate knee ligaments. An untypical way for a Stoke player to pick up an injury – in that there aren't so many winning goals to celebrate – but entirely typical in its farcical nature. It put him out for the rest of the season. Very bad news indeed. He was starting to look the complement that Bjarni required; they'd made the winning goal between them. Even the silver lining – that he would not imminently be sold to Cardiff – felt like no compensation.

Home crowds were steady at about 14,000, a figure that could be described as hopeless, about half the ground capacity and no improvement on the year before when we were a division lower. Ticket prices had gone up: this accounted for some of the missing. On top of that, the team were hardly setting the place on fire and there were no glamorous new signings of any note either: this accounted for some of the missing too. Access to the ground, by car or public transport isn't all it might be, but that's scraping for an excuse: people in Stoke can find excuses for inaction anywhere, which is more like a reason. For instance, following the opening match of the season at Hillsborough I went to a class reunion, at a pub across the way from my old school (the Hazlehurst Arms if you're ever looking for a session). I was on the road anyway, for the game, and I like driving, but all the same the detour I'd made to get there (from Norwich to Stoke via Sheffield) was large. There'd been an earlier plan to hold the do at a fancier venue about five miles away from the pub opposite the school, but some potential participants had complained that this was 'too far to travel'. I have to describe that attitude as symptomatic.

But on the other hand, there *is* a terminal malaise at the club, and because of it many ex-supporters, no matter how near or far they live, have been operating the boycott system for many years longer than I did.

What!? The twat (I hope somebody petrol bombs his house)

A few weeks after the school reunion, early on an October morning, Rob Moulton, a friend with whom I first attended Stoke matches by catching two buses there and two buses back, or walking when we didn't have the money, and with whom I'd become re-acquainted at the Hazlehurst, came off his nightshift in Stoke and called me on his mobile.

Have you heard the news, youth? he said.

No, I replied, wiping the sleep from my eyes. What?

'Steve Cotterill's resigned.'

'You're fucking joking.'

But he wasn't. Seconds later Graham Etherington was on the phone.

World War Three broken out, has it? Trezza enquired.

Cotterill stayed with us for thirteen games of a three-year contract. He arrived saying he had no doubt that coming to a club with a big history like Stoke was the right move for him. He talked about his passion, his loyalty, his hard work and about not being a quitter. Within moments of this base act of treachery, Steve Quitterill was one of the nicer rechristenings he acquired.

What had happened? Well, for a start, it was autumn. In the season of the mists of mellow fruitfulness, as surely as leaves fall from the trees, managers are kicked out of jobs. The situation the Quitter found himself in was that Sunderland, of the Premiership, following a poor start to *their* season, had sacked their gaffer. None of Quitterill's business, of course, except that he had been headhunted. Although it wasn't quite a like-for-like opportunity that landed on the table of his rented house on the outskirts of Stoke. With us he was manager; with them he would become second-in-command to the *actual* new manager and World's Most Boring Man, Howard Wilkinson – widely and unaffectionately known to fans at large as Sgt. Wilco. Prior to his appointment Wilco was to be found doing some unutterably dull pen-pushing at the FA. You can imagine Quitterill's dilemma: anyone could see how hard it would be to honour the remaining 87 per cent of his contract and continue building on the promise he was developing in our squad when instead he could be slinging his hook to run drill up in the north-east for the Sarge for thousands of pounds more a year. From the start he'd made in the Potteries he had every chance of establishing himself as a hero,[17] but that simply didn't come into it, because the north-east is a football hotbed full of big clubs, whereas in the north Midlands we struggle to half fill the stadium.

Two main strands of opinion emerged on *The Oatcake* messageboard that day. (I read it all, because when I wasn't watching 'Football Latest' to see the press conferences and the reaction, I was online. Working was out of the question.)

Strand One opinion, and I'm going to put this as nicely as possible, was that Cotterill was a cunt. They're a strange breed, managers, they come and they go, as everybody knows. Everybody knows the dice are loaded, everybody rolls with their fingers crossed. Everybody knows the war is over, everybody knows the good guys lost. Everybody knows. That's how it goes. Everybody knows.

Everybody knows. But Lt Lance Quitterill's behaviour lacked the smallest nugget of integrity. I found myself wholly in agreement with Strand One.

Strand Two: well, there is something profoundly wrong at the top of SCFC. Everybody knows. A club of our size has no business languishing in the third tier of English football for the four consecutive years (and very nearly a fifth) that preceded this. It's much, much worse than embarrassing, it's utterly and

---

17 Aside from beginning to do well within the limitations of our squad and demonstrating an instinct towards attacking football, there was a clenched-fist gesture he made to us when he came out of that oddly situated tunnel at Burnley which looked good, made the right sort of impression, bonding-wise.

compellingly inept. The kindest interpretation of Cunterill's decision in choosing demotion at Sunderland in the way he did is to assume that it had taken him just the thirteen games to reach the realization that he would be banging his head against the wall for years to come so long as the hierarchy was constituted in the way that it was: i.e. with Peter Coates and Keith Humphreys on the board.

These two are – I hesitate over the choice of word here – 'our' (they belong to us? I suppose they do) longest-standing directors, grocers with fingers in several meat and potato and chicken balti pies. Stadia catering and online and highstreet betting, amongst others activities, form an operating base (I'm anxious not to lose any more money to them than I have to, hence I select my bookies with care and lose my money to villains I don't know). They are fossilized businessmen of the seventies school – self-satisfied, condescending, patronizing – who take out of the club whilst at the same time neglecting to invest in it. Occasionally they make a loan at a slightly more favourable rate than a bank might. They're individuals for whom improving the team by shelling out on those expensive liabilities, players, goes totally against the grain. Their ambition does not stray beyond the obvious: the Rolex, the mulitplex on the Costa. Unlike Waddo, they really do need gold Bentleys to impress the ladies. If they have any motivation for remaining at the club beyond the possibility of profit-taking, it's for the aggrandizement that goes with the position, the glory of a seat in the directors' box, even if it's a seat in the away section of the directors' box at Colchester United. Power is still power even when it's applied in an unpowerful and humiliating environment. By some sleight of hand – the use of those quaintly algebraic transferrable A and B preference votes so beloved of sitting charlatans, by which means ultimate blocking-veto is retained without the requirement to take commensurate responsibility – they'd stitched things up beautifully at the time of the Icelandic 'takeover' to the net effect that they remain where they are in perpetuity. Or forever, depending who dies first, Us, the Club or Them. The money we invest at the gate goes into the black hole of their non-existent ambition. Walking across the wasteland to the stadium, it's tempting to think of chucking your notes straight into the adjacent incinerator and cutting out the middle men.

The Icelandics hold the majority stake, the 60-odd per cent they purchased which allowed Coates and Humphreys to walk away with £3.5 million. Or rather, to stay put with £3.5 million. By most reckonings this price was over the odds, the deal being made at the top of a buoyant market which has since crashed, and for sure they failed to get promotion quickly enough. That's football when you don't know what you're doing, but you'd have to say they had a decent slice of luck in escaping the Second Division in the season they began asset stripping in earnest by flogging our best players to Cardiff. All the same, their lack of success since they started their adventure means they are too skint now to be able to manoeuvre. They are about £7 million in debt. They'd sell up if they could. Unfortunately, they don't own the new ground, they rent it from a group made up of two development companies and Stoke-on-Trent City

Council. So the prime requirement for a sale – title of the freehold asset of the land and buildings – isn't on offer. Just the debt, the players, the staff, the wage bill and the SCFC brand name. A hot oatcake it ain't. From observation, I'd say the Icelandics aren't on speaking terms with the grocers.

This is the background that translates to a fast-quitting manager and thousands of stay-away punters. Expert excuse-finders though we may be, there's no shortage of them in this depressing scenario.

Q. How can you build a successful football team in the absence of aspiration?

A. You cannot.

Q. And why should people from the low-pay culture which this shower help to maintain cough up their hard-earned to watch the results of their anti-enterprise?

A. No reason whatsoever.

When I caught up with Jack later that day, he had not heard the Quitting News. The comings and goings at Stoke City were not the talking point in Norwich that they would be back in the Midlands. In attempting an explanation as to why (Why Dad, *why*?) I briefed him about the board. It wasn't something we'd discussed much before, it's not the normal concern of a teenage boy. A teenage boy dreams of playing for his club, not of sitting in a directors' box watching complacently on, deaf to the opinions of the proletariat.

After giving me a hearing, it was clear that the minutiae of the dealings of boring old men remained outside the scope of his interest. His reaction to events was exactly the same as it was before my summary – his focus centred entirely on Cotterill's appalling lack of honour – and his precise and repeated verbal response provides the title of this passage, and remains unchanged, and I don't blame him. The blame lies elsewhere.

Wanderers

Ben Keane, supplier of tickets for Norwich matches, those tickets I decline on account of travelling coast-to-coast to Preston North End, friend, advisor and counsellor (you don't think I get through this without help do you?), travelled with us to our first managerless game, at our place, against Wolverhampton. A big match, Wolves are an old and local enemy – I remember stabbed bodies being passed over my head in encounters against them during take-our-end type-situations in the mid-seventies. Ben had, of course, heard detailed reports about the Stoke City experience on many occasions and the moment had come for him to see it for himself.

A few weeks later we found ourselves in the Orgasmic bar in Norwich where Ben was responding, after an appropriate period of time for reflection had elapsed, to his day out.

We'd had an easy journey, and so, with a little time on our hands, I gave him a quick pre-match tour. First stop, a favourite of mine for any guest to my hometown, was the site of the old Victoria Ground in the old Stoke town centre. It's six years since we moved the mile or so to the Britannia. Were Stoke-on-Trent a remotely sorted-out, vibrant, thriving, vivacious or normal place, this location would by now be the site of a mixed retail, residential and commercial development. Or maybe a cinema complex, or an exhibition hall, or an arts venue. Or *something*. As it is, it's a field of weeds and litter, with an obelisk of concrete stepping still remaining at the old Boothen End giving clue to its former life. It's owned by some relic from the old board who picked it up for zip when we were moved from our proper home and who has done fuck-all with it. That's how it goes. Everybody knows.

Extraordinary, Ben said at the time. Property redevelopment forms part of his work as a solicitor. He hadn't progressed beyond his initial impression on this one. The dereliction is a sight that provokes head-shaking in the casual (or, in my case, the uncasual) observer. We both shook our heads at the time, and once more, in honour of the memory, we shook them in the bar.

After the ex-Victoria Ground we moved along to the city centre itself, which isn't a place called Stoke, it's a place called Hanley, a mile or so away from the ex-Victoria Ground in the opposite direction to the Britannia. But, and this struck Ben sharply, there *isn't* a city centre. This is because Stoke-on-Trent is a conurbation of six towns. It sprawls, like LA. Unlike LA, it has grown in a wholly piecemeal fashion – any style of architecture can, and will, be given planning permission to be built next to any other style of architecture and most of this is of the cheap and brutal variety. It looks like there's been a war.

It's a landscape that didn't require a nuclear winter to acquire the nuclear-wintered look. Actually, maybe it's *not* so unlike LA.

We came across an espresso bar. At four in the afternoon it was just closing (the Wolves game was a 5.30 kick-off). Espresso was off. Hold the front page: Stoke *is* unlike LA.

They've got espresso bars here, then, said Ben, in a bemused and slightly disorientated manner that I took to mean: What sort of espresso bar closes at four in the afternoon then? There's something fishy going on, isn't there? For example: this truck I see parked in the (so far as you can tell) Main Street with people performing karaoke from the back. What is the meaning of that?

I didn't think it right to attempt any answers at this point, I thought it best to allow the general impression to sink in, and regarding the karaoke truck, I don't have an answer. Every time I go down Main Street it's there. I have no idea why – there isn't a crowd, there's absolutely no interest and there's no tune either. Maybe they're Fail supporters who've found a better way to spend their time than watching their awful 'team'.

We entered a clothes store in pursuit of our two charges who had temporarily escaped us in pursuit of Burberry headwear. The shop was on three floors. We described the boys to a shopgirl and asked if she'd seen them, which she hadn't, and then we caught sight of them on a CCTV monitor. Watch out for those two, I said, They're shoplifters. I'm no stand-up, but my delivery was such that this was supposed to be a joke. It was taken seriously and caused momentary alarm. I wondered about this on the walk back to the car as we were passing the karaoke truck for the final time (I think I saw Robbie Williams). She should have known I was attempting humour, shouldn't she, I asked.

No question, Ben replied. Look at that, he said, pointing to the ugliest prefabricated concrete-clad tower block you'll ever see. If a child accidentally knocked over a multi-storey car park and hastily re-assembled the bits in the hope that nobody would notice, this building would be the result. He laughed a little, more or less to himself, as if he thought he might be getting the hang of things.

Ben was further stimulated at the match itself, not least because not only is Stoke so *not* LA, it *so isn't* Norwich either. I mean, our crowd. As he said in the Orgasmic: 'I formed the impression that I was not going to find myself sitting next to the Professor of Gender Studies. The Hornbyesque, gentrified type of supporter that you might find at Carrow Road was distinguished by his absence, no?'

No indeed. That's right, I replied.

'But the madmen around us, they were superb entertainment in themselves, weren't they?'

Yes, I said. We really do have some magnificent headbangers. We also have the old lady Pearly Queens of the enamel-badge-encrusted scarf. We have the undisputed possessor of the World's Finest (if this is the apt adjective to apply) Mullet. We have the Pissed-Up Nutter-in-a-Filthy-Dirty-Hat, a man who thinks the rest of us do not sing enough and bangs on the back of the stand explaining his thoughts as follows: 'Sing up the Boothen, c'mon, *sing*, y'fuckin bastards.' The crowd as a whole is characterized by the synchronized throbbing of forehead-veins. Sitting in the River End at Carrow Road one Saturday afternoon (when Stoke were playing on a Sunday) I was astonished when the man behind me asked me to sit down as I stood out of my seat as play was approaching and a goal looked likely. I mean *really*. This person was supposed to *support* Norwich, and I *don't*, and *I* was more excited than *him*. I can't see this happening at Stoke.

The violence amused me, Ben went on.

There'd been a small bit of fighting and a huge police presence. Apparently very many knives and fireworks had been confiscated (from *Wolves*, not from *us*). We confessed we'd enjoyed the aggro, that it had added to the excitement of a not very good game. As we'd walked away post-match we'd agreed that we found women PCs in riot kit sexually attractive.

This chant, he went on, We are Stoke, We are Stoke, We are Stoke . . .

Yes, I said.

It's quite extraordinarily basic, isn't it?

Yes, I said.

Sensational, he said.

Yes, I said.

But when you add it all together, he said, the derelict ex-ground, the lack of a city centre, the fighting, the police helicopter (the Hoolicopter) circling overhead, the terrible team – we lost 2–0 – the karaoke van – what does it all say about Stoke? What, he went on, attempting to come to some sort of conclusion, would people from Stoke say if you asked them what it was about Stoke that made them proud to be from Stoke? If people from Manchester might say the music scene, the nightlife, all the great Manchester bands, Old Trafford, Maine Road, or if Liverpudlians might say the cultural melting pot, the Walker, the Tate, all the great bands, Anfield, Bill Shankly, etc, what would people from Stoke say?

'It's a disaster of a place with a disaster of a football club (not to mention The Fail)'?

That the people are really friendly, I replied (fighting apart) and that if your chances of scoring an espresso are low, the Bovril at the Brit isn't so bad.

We sipped from our lime and sodas. It wasn't enough of an answer for Ben. And it wasn't enough of an answer for me.

And neither was the performance good enough either. Nowhere near. In a fashion that can sometimes happen with highly paid professional sportsmen, confidence had departed with the Quitter. If we chanted *Stevie Cotterill, You're a wanker, You're a wanker*, for the benefit of both the Sky cameras and ourselves, we did it pretty half-heartedly, a reflection of how the team played. This defeat marked the beginning of an impressive losing streak and confirmed what many of us instinctively felt – that in heading towards mid-table mediocrity, the Quitter had been overachieving. The human resources out there on the pitch, the boys who had fluked us up into this division, one division below where we think we rightly belong, weren't actually up to the job of keeping us in it. The fourth of the defeats took place a cold Wednesday night.

Long day's journey into nowt

Though the decision to travel to Stoke and back in the chilly midweek to see a game against Watford on the wind-blasted hill next to the incinerator was a late one, it was not difficult to make: even on a three-match run of defeats characterized by performances of outstanding ineptness, for at least one of us, there was still the happy prospect of missing the first (double) period (of chemistry) the next day.

Once in Stoke the evening started well, our car park man lifting up a chain to allow us into the hotel car park adjacent to the actual car park for which he takes his four quid, which was full. Dunner worry surry, I'll sort thee iyt, he said, in the strongest of local vernaculars as he arranged this convenience. While I admire this man's attitude Jack admires his accent. *Dunner worry*, he was saying to himself, *Dunner worry*, as we walked towards the ticket office, outside of which we were apprehended by another excellent person who was eager to divest himself of a couple of complimentaries for the main stand, free of charge. Got more tickets than I know what to do with, youth, he said. Nine times out of ten the story is that the man's wife knows Terry Conroy's sister. Terry Conroy was on the wing in the class of '72.

The free seats were next to the directors' box[18] which was where we were planning to sit that night anyway, so the excellent man's intervention was even more excellent than he knew. Normally we sit behind our goal, but George Burley, the recently sacked manager of Ipswich Town, recently of the Premiership, was supposed to be appearing as a prelude to replacing the Quitter. The directors' box is a fenced-off area where they afford themselves the luxury of cushioned seats on which to complacently sit. I thought a close-up of the blunderers in so-called charge of our club was overdue. Also, we'd lost 4–0 the Saturday before to Rotherham.[19] I couldn't imagine much atmosphere in the new Boothen End on a midweek fixture against Watford following a distressing result like that, and anyway, a decent perspective would make a nice change: the foreshortening you get from behind the goal means that, howl though you will in protest at decisions which go against you in the opposite penalty area, you really have no idea

---

18 They were also next to a classic season-ticket-holding Mr Bean. A short, overtly verbal example with an extraordinary range of contradictory opinions on everything happening both on and off the pitch and in the whole wide world too. Jack sat next to him in the first half. He was like a rat up a drainpipe in getting back to our seats after half-time to make sure it was *me* who sat next to him in the second half. Jack had been badgering me to acquire season tickets, on the argument we were not hardcore enough supporters without them. This man allowed me to rest my case vis-à-vis the dangers involved.

19 As I predicted earlier – an unhappily accurate forecast made unhappier by my not having a tenner on it, although I wouldn't, of course, because I never ever bet against my team, profitable though this would be.

what happened. You only have an accurate view of what's going on in the near half of the field. Of course your own end is easily the best place to be in the sense of emotional involvement – you get less than zero atmosphere in most main stands; ours is specialised in the sense that you get less than zero investment there either. If that.

Ipswich Town, Burley's ex-employers, are a compact and prosperous club in a compact and prosperous market town beneath the wide skies of East Anglia. Ipswich's population, at about 150,000, is less than half of Stoke's. Ipswich sell 19,000 season tickets, we sell 6,000. Ipswich have been competently run by businessman David Sheepshanks, a chairman with a football media profile and an understanding of how a club should, ideally, relate to its citizens. Sheepshanks knows that good public relations requires the kind of pronouncement that goes: Promotion to the Premiership is worth £20 million pounds to the local economy. This is a message of the type that alerts the whole business community to the idea that to invest in the success of the club is to invest in the success of themselves. So it's not just the season tickets; the advertising, the sponsorship, the whole corporate package sells out too.

Burley entered our directors' box and made himself uncomfortable amongst the two factions of our critically split board, the grocers to his left, the Icelandics to his right. As he sat squirming between them it was impossible for him not to pick up on their total lack of communication and commonality of purpose.

As he looked out, this is what he saw:

1) A thoroughly disenchanted support and not many of them at that: 11,000, a *less* than half-full house, under 4 per cent of the local population.

2) A great deal of cold dark night.

Why, he thought to himself, are the corners of this stadium not filled in? It's a common enough condition in older grounds, but rather less so in new-builds. For instance Reading's Madejski Stadium is a smart, contained bowl, the same applies to Derby's Pride Park and Leicester's Walkers Stadium and others. Is it because rectangular buildings are inexpensive and easy to construct, whereas curved bits linking the rectangles together are a lot more costly? Does this club invest in quality, or does it prefer knocking things up on the cheap, he asked himself. He glanced to the grocers. To his right sat Gunnar Thor Gislason, the chairman who had flown in from Reykjavik to meet him. He seemed a decent enough bloke. He was wearing a club anorak – nice for a visit to the training ground, but the appropriate garment to pull off the peg when presenting your highly rated new manager, himself sharply turned out in a cashmere Crombie, for the first time in public? No.

Is it possible that these Icelandics are as disconnected in cultural terms as they are geographically, George wondered. Not to mention their stinginess (the budget had been discussed). And with this combination – grocers, schism, out-of-touchness, lack of kronur – is it really possible to even begin to think about attracting the best sort of personnel, physios, dietitians, marketeers – not to mention actual players – to the place?

George looked to the pitch.

Here he saw a poor side playing appallingly in front of their new manager-to-be. Half an hour had gone by and they were already 2–0 down. The second of the goals had been the result of as hopeless a piece of collective defending as you could ever wish not to see. Even if despite this ineptitude there appeared to be a couple of decent players out there, there was no team. There was no team on the pitch because . . .

No prizes: there was no team in the director's box.

George's gaze returned to the cold night. I'm looking at 13,000 missing supporters, he thought. To bring them back is to buy half a squad at least, he thought, and the deal on the table here is that I've got nothing to spend. There have to be better job offers coming along than this, he thought.

It's only too easy to imagine the hotel room, the sleep on it, the close shave, the necessary phone call.

Typical Stoke in a nutshell

The club had arranged a morning press conference to introduce the new manager. It must have come late, Burley's call of regret, too late to stop the press from showing up anyway. In place of the unveiling of the new supremo we were treated to a first-class demonstration of how to remain calm in the face of a crisis. Due to unforeseen circumstances, in place of the advertised programme, we cut live to an improvised comedy involving a larger-than-life lady shoo-ing away a bemused media pack. Right, the lady was going, No press conference today, you'll all have to come back another time. The camera zoomed in on her ample rear quarters as, with all the determination of a prizewinning Collie, the lady rounded the hacks towards the exit saying, Sorry, but that's it: Now off you go! C'mon. The door's that way . . .

This brilliant display of media-handling took place in front of the traditional table set with the traditional water jugs and glasses in front of the traditional backdrop of panels bearing the traditional club crest and traditional sponsors logos. And in the traditional seats behind the traditional table sat nobody. A better advert would be hard to devise. I suppose they could've thrown in a few paralytic Prominents to really give it that finishing touch.

No chairman, director, or chief executive ever appeared to give an explanation, or even to test out some risible spin. It wasn't just piss-poor PR, it was active cowardice. Nice work comrades.

The following day, Friday, in a knee-jerk response to George's declination, a person called Tony Pulis, who applies for the job every time it becomes available, was announced as new manager. *Who are yer?* Nobody's ever heard of him, but research will show that he has been removed from the stewardship of Bournemouth, Gillingham, Bristol City and Portsmouth, and that many supporters of these clubs are at a loss to find a good word to say about him. Bristol City supporters actually chanted 'Pulis for Portsmouth' when his name was linked with the club he was about to cart off to. The bad words they have to say about him run along the lines that he's a long-ball merchant whose usual modus operandi is to sue the evicting club for wrongful dismissal once they've sacked him for being shit.

On Saturday we made it five reversals in a row by losing our first match under Pulis at Walsall. Walsall play in an awful little 'stadium' called the Bescot which is situated immediately underneath a raised section of the M6. It was sleeting rain. If the grey atmosphere inside the tinpot shack didn't already feel enough like a timewarp into a particularly grim seventies afternoon, for pre-match entertainment the MC played obscure Slade tracks on his dansette. Some of our fans demonstrated a phlegmaticism that I certainly couldn't muster. A man just in front of me ate a packed lunch out of a Tupperware box: this was not a venue in which I could stomach a picnic.

A group of others, as a comment on the Bescot, managed to get going a chorus of:

My garden shed,
my garden shed
Is bigger than this,
is bigger than this
My garden shed is bigger than this: it's got a door and four
*   windows, my garden shed is bigger than this.*

Though Jack found the singing highly amusing, he'd had more than enough of the team. Football is a game played in the boardroom. It's one of the oldest of the old footballing clichés. I'd had more than enough of the whole superb operation.

Pulis, a shifty looking individual, had a poor debut, taking off Bjarni when we were attempting a second-half comeback and Bjarni was just about the only hope we'd got. As a consequence, the first song with which we were obliged to greet the new manager was, *You don't know what you're doing.* He looked at us nastily, giving the impression of being the sort of stepfather who might just about find it within himself to be nice to you in front of your mum then beat you when her back was turned. This is grossly unfair. Nevertheless, it was how I felt. Unhappily he reminded me of a Jehovah's Witness who lived in our street when I was young and came round our house to accuse me of scratching his car with my scooter. That I was guilty was neither here nor there, he stood on our doorstep employing an unpleasant and threatening attitude while having it out with my mum. She could take care of herself, but I was just a kid. He frightened me and he knew it and you could see he knew it and you could see he liked knowing it. The world didn't end when he claimed it would, though for the next ninety minutes, with us going 3–0 down before finally losing 4–2, and only ever looking like a considerably worse outfit than *Walsall*, I felt like it might have been better if it had. Pulis stood on the touchline in the rain wearing a baseball cap with rain dripping from the peak. Otherwise he was attired à la Gudjon. Arsène Wenger he wasn't. For fuck's sake.

I left the miserable amphitheatre filled with nausea. I mean, I felt physically ill. I joined in with the ranters on Five Live's phone-in on the drive back and ranted my piece which helped not a jot.

Jack boycotted the next match. Me too, except I went anyway.

A November Saturday in the Midlands. 4.45 pm

Three grown men in replica shirts and jeans sit on the terracing of the new Boothen End in complete silence, heads hanging, shoulders drooped, a picture of abject despondence.

Not even as good as that shower, I remark, passing in front of them.

One looks up. It's not even easy to get to the ground, though, is it? he says.

An odd response, but easy to interpret, a mind-bubble that recognized the problem as absolute, total, complete, infrastructural, integrated, and long, long term. Nothing serves to illustrate your standing in the world more vividly than playing like Athletico Dog and Duck to lose at home to Grimsby in a relegation six-pointer and in the process exchange places with them to re-enter the bottom three.

And next week we play Portsmouth who are turning the race at the top of the table into a runaway. Which means all we have to look forward to in the immediate future is a roasting, a seventh straight defeat on the bounce my son.

The future's bright (not)

It's an awkward fixture down on the south coast in ways unconnected with the match itself. Jack's mum's new partner supports Portsmouth. Relations between us – Marion and I – are civilized, un-hostile, friendly even. She didn't run off and leave me for the Portsmouth fan, thank God (things are bad enough without me having to put up with that). Martin entered the scene after the parting. It's me who does the running off and leaving, not something I'm proud of. I thought we might improve on the generation that parented us by not involving ourselves in serial divorces, but the number of people I know who've managed it are far fewer than those who haven't. Jack and I drive to the match under separate cover from Marion and Martin who are attending in the home stand. We're bound to lose. It's only the insane supply of unfounded hope[20] that sees us travelling at all. In one of our habitual en-route conversations we analyze our entire squad and decide on our preferred starting line-up, formation and subs. The strikers from whom we can select are as follows: Cookie (as Honest as ever), Big Chris Iwelumo (his extreme tallness is his outstanding attribute, yet he is no great header of the ball, and

---

20 According to Nietzsche, the worst of all evils, because it prolongs the torments of man. I don't know how long it took him to come up with this, but a study of Stoke fans would've provided him with a short cut.

less good with his feet), the on-loan Mooney (Big Chris Iwelumo without the height) and Greenacre (the new signing, the one who was injured pre-season, the great prospect. We've seen him now, he looks more than a bit Honest). Any which way we line them up, we're not expecting to score.

And if you can't score, then the best you can do is take a point from a goalless draw. This is the nineteenth fixture of the season: the only clean sheet we've kept was the magnificent 0–0 on the opening day at Sheffield Wednesday, who are now down there at the bottom of the class with us. Sheffield Wednesday, it turns out, were the Fotherington-Thomas's of the Big Skool, boys who would more likely be found playing with gurls than kicking our bottoms. In each of the other eighteen games we have conceded at least one goal. In short, our defence is rotten. The midfield (Bjarni and, intermittently, the swan-like Hoekstra aside) is equally lousy. So the overview, back to front, is as follows:

The goalie hasn't kept a clean sheet for as long as he can remember, which in turn reflects badly on his defenders, who clearly aren't satisfying their job descriptions; the midfielders are as adept at supplying the front men as they are at protecting the back line, and the strikers couldn't land a dustbin lid into a main road.

That's why we lose every week, innit Dad.

Impossible to disagree.

My mates have even stopped taking the piss, it's too easy, he continues.

I wish that was hard to believe.

An atmosphere of chronic malaise permeates the car as we silently ruminate on this iniquitous situation. The mood begins to lift only as our discourse resumes and moves on to less painful subject matter, i.e. the hip-hop scene and related areas. I query Jack about the meaning of a word that I've been hearing amongst his massive. It may be that everybody else in the world already knows what it means, but I've missed out. The word is 'blingin'. The way I've overheard it, I've taken it to mean good, like 'bad' used to. Its precise meaning turns out to be much more specific and appertains to these characters you see about the streets who have very many heavy chains and pennants hanging round their necks, displayed on the outside of their sweatshirts. They are blingin. The more, and the heavier, the jewellery, the more they bling. Except, according to Jack, you can't actually 'bling' (it's not a verb) you can only 'be blingin' (it's a stand-alone adjective). That's sorted that out then, at least the day won't be a total waste of time. The long hours that we spend together on the road allow for the sort of exchange we might not otherwise get round to. And the silences we might not otherwise get round to either. Though obviously I shouldn't use the word at all, I know I won't be able to help myself because it's a word I like. At least now I'm briefed I won't be using it erroneously, innit, thereby giving his mates some more way-too-easy piss-taking opportunities. Bling bling. The Pompey Chimes.

The away end at Portsmouth is as thoroughly unpleasant a venue as anywhere in the United Kingdom (the Bescot aside), distinguished by crumbling concrete steps, the absence of a roof, a toilet which would not be out of place in a Greek island airport, and a salmonella shanty shack staffed by acned lobotomy victims. There *are* seats to sit on. I've overheard people at literary soirées bemoaning seated ends; you can still find the romantic mindset abroad which imagines that suffering-through-standing conveys the authentic old working-class footy day out. This idea tends to carry weight most amongst those who follow successful sides, who perhaps get to stand nostalgically once a year at an away FA Cup tie, provided that television hasn't persuaded the underdog club to switch to the bigger club's ground for the money. Maybe it allows them to experience a nice feeling of marginality and underprivilegedness that they can't get from the performance of their team on the pitch. The seating at Fratton Park's away end is bolted to the old standing terracing. The front few rows are therefore located *below* the level of the perimeter retaining wall. When standing was the order of the day here you'd have had a worm's eye-view. To watch the game from these seats (where our tickets were allocated, for which you do actually have to pay actual money) you'd have to be the kind of worm who could jump. From the seated position you are afforded a sight of a mere *portion* of the pitch: the middle portion, which is a hill. I suppose that could help us, the hill. Our motto[21] might easily be *Everest, the Hard Way*. We're hardly selling out

---

21 Laughably, in the light of recent events, *Vis Unita Fortior* — United Strength is Stronger.

away any more, so, after sampling the pleasures of Row A during the warm-up, and messing about by trying to identify players by the tops of their heads, we moved on up to the numerous free seats further back in the stand.

We moved on up and we kept on wishing: Hush now child, and don't you cry.

At five o'clock, with our heroes on the wholly predictable wrong end of the 3–0 score – the hill, needless to say, played against us – we found ourselves prevented from leaving the luxury facilities of the paddock because outside the police were dispersing several hundred mixed members of the N40 and the 6.57 gangs.[22]

The temperature rises quickly in these situations. Our young supporters vent their spleen at the 6.57, instead of at their own custodians, where it more properly belongs; our mature supporters address stewards about civil rights in a non-too-civil manner. Those superhumans who *still* retain a sense of humour sing a song at a warming-down Pompey substitute, querying the wisdom of his avant-garde haircut. With Jack's mum making her way round to collect her little angel for a night out with some rapturous table-topping Portsmouth people (oh

---

22 Portsmouth Prominents. The 6.57 was the first fast train to Waterloo from the harbour station. The earlier train was a slow-stopping one. The 6.57 gang caught the train in question to away matches, particularly up north. It was used extensively during the time of the great Persil voucher give away. Buy one ticket, get one free.

joy), I stand contemplating a fog-bound 200-mile drive home on my lonesome ownsome (if our outward-bound journeys have the flavour of going away on holiday, the returns are often worse than coming back from Spain on a wet Thursday afternoon). Jack kicks at the perimeter wall. Silently we await our release: Grumpysson feat. Grump Diddy, the most hacked-off double-hander anywhere on the planet, followers of an entirely bling-free team of non-blingin' tossers.

No one likes them, they're not here, and soon enough we won't be either

Millwall fans share headline billing with us. Their Prominent supporters being at least as prominent as ours, they found themselves banned from our ground, as we will be from theirs later in the season. We smuggled one in, Jack's badass, blingin' friend the Hozzmeister, who kept his head down, which was the best idea. He missed nothing, though Millwall *did* score in the first minute, whereas we didn't score at all. Eight defeats in a row. It's seventeen years since we managed this level of consistency: in the mid-eighties we established a jewel amongst records – as the club to be relegated from the old First Division with the lowest number of points *ever* under the new *three* points for a win system, which is to say we had attained such expertise at losing that we were 33 per cent worse than any team had ever been under the old *two* points for a win system. If compound fractional analysis is applied, I believe that made us two-thirds worse than anything in history. Certainly our stats for that season were awe-inspiring. We went down with the worst overall record ever posted in the Football League, watched by our lowest crowds for a quarter of a century. The 1984–5 season was a meltdown year from which we've never recovered. We have not returned to the top flight since. This was the logical end of a freefall sequence that began a decade earlier when a storm blew the lid off a stand at the old Victoria Ground. The directors – antecedents of the grocers – had neglected to arrange adequate insurance cover. This came as a surprise to supporters. I imagine the only surprise to the board was that the negligent dereliction with which they went about their duties was exposed. In the interests of construction work the great Waddo was forced to sell the finest elements of his fine team, piece by piece, until eventually, as the winter snow thawed on the new roof, there was nothing left.

A slip-up on the road to greatness (& bastards in black)

In the next match away at Gillingham we brought the losing streak to an end with a 1–1 draw. Which was a shame for a couple of reasons:

1) because you want to end a sequence like that with an unlikely 6–0 away win that can be featured and highlighted with

a manager and/or player interview on Five Live for your enjoyment on your drive back; and

2) because in the following week at home to Coventry (who are absolute crap) we lost again.

Without the hiccup at Gillingham – and my feeling by this stage was that the single point gained would turn out to be of no consequence, that we were definitely going straight back down – we could have been looking at establishing a new all-comers record for defeats. As it was, we could only add the eight-in-a-row to our B-list statistics:

Second-oldest League club. (As founder members of the Football League we finished bottom in the first two seasons and lost our place.)

Runners-up only to Rochdale in lifetime underachievement in the FA Cup.

109 years in existence before playing in a Wembley final.

Lost 5–1 to Oxford after Oxford hadn't scored a goal for eight hours or something.

Windiest stadium. (It's even windy in the concourses underneath the stands. It takes a special kind of genius to incorporate that design feature.)

It was a bleak draw at Gillingham too, though it was at least enlivened by the finest chairman's programme column I've ever read. A normal chairman's programme column gives the word 'blah' a bad name: Blah blah blah blah blah, we thank you for your continuing support. Our chairman seldom even bothers to pick his pencil up, leaving it to the chief executive to give us little lectures about our behaviour and to explain how difficult it is to run a business as demanding as a football club. Gillingham are ex-employers of Tony Pulis. Here is an extract of what the Gills' chairman, Mr Paul Scally, had to say in welcoming Mr Pulis back:

> I have no interest in Pulis or what he does with his life. For me, he was the most evil, vindictive and malicious person I have ever met or worked with, but I have long been over that unhappy stage of my life and I am now again very focused on the club and happy in my private life.

Private life? There was a further page in the same spirit. In the accompanying (full-length) picture Scally displays the quintessential style sense of the short one in an end-of-pier comedy double-act. In contradistinction to this disparaging material, Pulis received a warm(ish) reception from the Gillingham crowd. Though I was by no means beginning to warm to him myself, these goings-on made me wonder whether, despite his mediocre touchline garb and his inability to inspire the team to win a game of football, he might not be as grim a specimen as I suspected. Anybody who is capable of provoking invective of that sort can't be all bad.

The following game, the defeat to Coventry (who are absolute crap), was distinguished by a command performance from an official who was making a record attempt of his own: Worst Referee in History. Mr Andy Hall sent off two of our players for nothing at all whatsoever and cautioned hundreds more from both teams, my favourite of which was the booking given to opposing player-manager Gary McAllister for ironic applause. 'Ironic applause' comes under subsection C, Appendix XIII of 'things to be on the lookout for' in the *Fifa Guide to Being a Total Arse for Today's Man in the Middle*. It's just before 'Gave me a funny look', and just after, 'Sported unconvincing goatee'.

For invading the pitch to stick his tongue out at Mr Hall, the club issued one of our fans with a life ban. Can't say fairer than that.

It's more or less impossible for any single entrant to triumph outright in the category of Worst Ever Ref though, because there's always another contender coming along wearing too-tight shorts and a sickly smile. We'll never forget the professional who, in an unimportant match like the '72 FA Cup semi-final against Arsenal, confused an ice-cream seller who was wearing a white apron (we were playing in our white away strip) with one of our defenders, thereby waving through an Arsenal player who was miles offside to score the winning goal. To borrow the expression made memorable by J. P. McEnroe (how I wish any of our players possessed a quarter of his passion and ability), they are all, in one way or another, the pits of the world.

A brilliant idea brilliantly conceived and executed

In the first scheme of its kind applied to supporters of a Football League club, and in vintage kick-'em-when-they're-down style, the hierarchy announced that in an effort to stamp on the Prominent situation once and for good, fans who wished to follow their team away from home would have to subscribe to a membership project. To join this required the filling in and returning of a form, and in addition providing the following evidence: two passport photos, two original forms of proof of address, or just a photocopy of a birth certificate in the case of a child (this is true), and ten English pounds, or just a fiver for a child (this is also true). In the event that you had never been in trouble with the police anywhere near a football ground ever before and had always cleaned your teeth, you would (allowing a minimum of fourteen days for processing) be issued with a cheap and nasty plastic card without which you would not be allowed to enter the away section of a Football League ground for any match involving Stoke City.

Why us?

Because the total number of arrests that occur when we play (extravagantly bumped up as a consequence of lunatic policing in local matches against The Fail) occasionally make the front pages and are the main story about the club.

Why so?

Because SCFC is otherwise so atrociously run and has such

abysmal PR[23] that it fails to make any impact on the back pages, and as a consequence contributes nothing to civic pride and much too little to the local economy.

Can it really be the case that when, for example, Man United play Leeds United in a Lancashire–Yorkshire confrontation in front of 60,000 that there is no associated trouble of the fighting kind? Of course not. Cuts, bruises and broken bones are a normal consequence of the collateral activity that surrounds these games. Do we get a big song and dance about that? Hardly. Life had been lost this season in city-centre trouble prior to a match in Burnley against Nottingham Forest. For all our bad reputation, there's never been a death associated with our hooligans. Are supporter ID schemes being instituted at Burnley and Forest? No. Why not? Because these clubs are of municipal and economic importance to their communities, and the vested interests at the Rotarians and the Masons and the Chambers of

---

23 A few years ago the industrialist Sir John Harvey-Jones in his television series *Troubleshooter* – in which he analyzed and suggested ways of improving ailing businesses – tackled a pottery manufacturer in Stoke. At one point he found his way up some back stairs to the 'office' where the 'design team' resided. A couple of forgotten part-time ladies laboured in a corner drawing up new patterns under 60-watt lightbulbs. They would occasionally receive a visit from the management who invariably dismissed their too-modern ideas as out of keeping with the firm's failing brand identity – more or less everything the company produced was of the brown-with-flowers variety. Harvey-Jones enquired how much was being spent on design. On learning it was a figure under £10,000 a year he shook his head and laughed and adjourned to the pub for a couple of pints. The Stoke City attitude to PR is from the same mould as the pottery company's to design: it's a weird and unnecessary new-fangled gimmick which they refuse to invest in or to take seriously.

STEPHEN FOSTER

Commerce apply the relevant pressure to the local press to ensure these stories are massaged down and the police don't make a big fuss because they too are fully in the loop, and the idea of a self-wounding proposal like our True Supporter's Card isn't even a prospect. Yes, it really is called that. Without the card you are not a True Supporter. Fans who've followed the team for half a century or more – or even youngsters like me who've only been at it for thirty years – may have managed to be True Supporters without needing to purchase a card to prove it up to now, and may have managed this without acquiring a police record as well, but not any more. Still, I guess when we sit down and think about it, we'll come to realize that a True Supporter's card is just what we've always wanted, it's simply that we haven't been able to recognize it ourselves until we've had it foist upon us. The naming of this shitty piece of plastic is a first-class example of their PR expertise. If it's anything (other than a howling own-goal) it's an Away Travel Card, and that's what it should be called. It's an Away Travel Card that has been introduced by incompetents and has been incompetently named. But what else should we expect? If the Icelandics knew how English business culture worked, they'd know where the Lodge[24] was and would have integrated themselves. If the grocers weren't entirely self-serving they'd have introduced the Icelandics to the ways of our world and none of this would be happening.

---

24 I don't like it, but that's how it goes. If I owned the club it would stick in my craw to have to get involved with these antique systems of manipulation, but, I hope, in the first instance anyway, I'd suppresss my repulsion and get *realpolitik* about it.

A typical fans' message from *The Oatcake* messageboard on the day of the announcement:

runcornade
ID CARDS . . . I'VE JUST ABOUT HAD ENOUGH
a little history, i'm 37 years old, live in runcorn, been everywhere with stoke home and away for years and years. i am really disillusioned with everything about my club. at first in the 70s i had dreams of europe, even championships. eighties i had lost the above dreams and realistically dreamed of winning a cup. nineties and dreams of getting in the premiership. 21st century i have no dreams because none of them are EVER EVER going to happen. i can't go on watching a team when all they are interested in is staying in business. which is true. what is the point? we sell all our best players – arrrgh i can't go on.
    and now they want to charge us 10 pounds just for the privilege of watching my team play. sorry but this is the last straw. what is it supposed to achieve anyway. get stuffed stoke that's all i can say.
    get stuffed.

And to put the raspberry on top of runcornade's list of woe, it's not as though investing your wages and dedicating wodges of leisure time to watch the Potters is a constructive activity, is it? The £10 (fiver for babes in arms) Incompetence Tax is being levied, let's not forget, to allow us the privilege of travelling this green and pleasant land in order to witness how many different ways there are to *lose*, with our interesting variants on the game of association football. A football club is the only type of enterprise that could treat its clients like this and have any hope of retaining their patronage, because such a club's core client-loyalty is effectively signed in blood. And to give them credit, the Incompetents are competent enough to know it.

Still and still, they don't care about results. The chairman recently announced that, post-TV deal collapse, there's not much *financial* difference between the First Division and the Second Division, thereby accidentally signalling that there's nothing in it for them to put a proper team on the pitch, because that would have only a marginal bearing on the performance of Stoke Holding SA. Well, Mr Chairman, I'm only a dimwitted True Supporter, but I beg to differ. Can it possibly be the case that if the cast of even a poor Premiership team like Aston Villa played for Stoke then the ground would not be full? The answer to this is, No. The cash through the gate for the sell-outs – the 15,000 extra supporters at £20 each – would bring in £300,000 per home game. There are twenty-three home games a season. That's an extra £6.5 million per trading year through the turnstiles without even taking into account the hike you could justify on the entrance fee. Nor is it allowing for a cup run. Or even two cup runs. Not to mention the knock-on boost to merchandise and catering and bumping up the price of car parking and everything else, et cetera. Et cetera, et cetera, et cetera.

If we had a better team, we would be richer. And if we

were richer, we'd have a better team. It's a Catch-22 (a full squad).

But the chairman is *financially* correct about this True Supporter's Card (yes, it really is called this, just in case the first time, even with the qualifying notes and accompanying exasperation, it might *still* have looked like a typo). He's not, as it were, wrong, anyway, in this specific sense: clubs receive no money from the opposition gate in League matches, so there's no pecuniary advantage whatsoever whether five, fifty, 500, or 5,000 of us follow the team away. Fewer will travel, it's inevitable. Many, like *runcornade*, will quite properly decline the last straw, and our debasement will continue and the opposition support will turn up the volume on the chant:

> *Is that all, is that all,*
> *Is that alll,*
> *you take away?*
> *Is that allll yoou take away?*

And sadly the answer will be, Yes, this is all we take away.

Because no person who hasn't registered and provided a copy of a gas bill and stumped up the cash and waited the minimum fourteen days for processing (i.e. no ordinary person) will be able to make the old-fashioned casual decision upon waking on a Saturday morning to cadge a lift in a mate of a mate's car to go and watch Stoke play in Bradford or

Nottingham or Birmingham, or even in a different part of Stoke itself – the ghetto where Port Vale are situated.

And all that will remain will be those few who are prepared to take whatever drops on them from a great height, a sort of faeces-coated cadaver of the ghost of a support, and even 'Delilah' will be sung pianissimo due to the pitiful shortfall in the voices of the choir:

> *At break of the day when that man drove away I was*
> *waiting,*
> *Whoawhoawhoawhoa*
> *I crossed the street to her house and she opened the door,*
> *Whoawhoawhoawhoa:*
> *She stood there laughing*
> *Hahahaha*
> *I put my dick in her hand*
> *And she laughed no more.*

Is it any surprise that the gaiety has stopped?

How funny is it?

So: *well done* board. A good day's work: give yourselves a pat on the back. And *well done* admin too: just to give the whole fabulous project the finishing touch, the box on the form where you enter your place of birth is one character too short to fit these words and hyphens: Stoke-on-Trent. I think we all know whose dick is in whose hand here. To call them wankers would be to denigrate the creative activity of onanists.

Crime and punishment

It's no easy walk being a father. Your ideal for yourself is to be rational, knowledgeable and grown up, rich but modest, amusing yet serious-minded, adorable and approachable while yet being tough but also kind. Sometimes you fall far short of your ideal. Our generation of dads like to think of themselves as mates to their children. That's the way I see it, at least, and I hear it from other parents, and I observe it too. It's an attitude I believe is, at least in part, a reaction against the emotional distance that could typify our own relationships with our own fathers just a generation ago, fathers who often worked long hours in manual jobs and were exhausted most of the time. I remember my dad leaving the house at six in the morning and returning home thirteen hours later having spent his day working on a road bridge somewhere near Manchester. He'd have a bite to eat and then go out 'on a foreigner'. A foreigner was a private job outside the firm. He would return at about midnight and be up again for six the following morning to do it all all over again. He worked most weekends too – he has no interest in football. (Nice try Pops.) It was common amongst my friends that their fathers worked these hours too; it was hardly a surprise that the regular state of a dad at the day's end was comatose. He could not help but be emotionally distant under those conditions.

You barely knew who he was as you studied him in close-up,

looking up his nose, where hairs grew, in fascinated horror as he dozed in the armchair, til your mum pulled you away by the ear whispering, *Sshh, your dad's asleep.* You wondered how he could possibly manage it at the epicentre of the din of snoring. And then, to get things going when he woke up, he might be reminded that he owed you a slippering for some crime or another that you'd forgotten you'd ever committed. *I'm gonna get whipped when my dad gets home!* was the standard sign-off as you took your leave of your mates. You could scarper out of it, though, if you were quick. It wasn't such a big deal and I wouldn't put it down as blame, really, either – you got six-of-the-best at school too: it was just the way it was, but, like drinking and driving, it's not an acceptable idea any more. And when you think back, it becomes even less of an acceptable idea now you've got kids of your own. But outside of that general scene, and even if things were relaxed on the beatings front and your father was a progressive on the emotional side and spoke to you sometimes and knew your name, there was a different tone, I think. We had to seek our fathers out, whereas we seek our children out. I think you could say that and believe it. I could, anyway.

The world has changed, more often than not *we* don't work the physical shifts that were normal back then, our hours can be more flexible, we have more time to reflect, and we live in a more reflective society. I think you could say that and believe it too.

Young people today have an easy life and they have no respec' for their elders. You could say this for sure.

It's a generalization which Jack is likely to confirm by replying:

Yeah, right Dad – *whatever,*

if I put the idea to him in *whatever* form of words.

He's coming on fifteen now and these are the years of the break. The biological relationship into which we are locked has an unpleasant built-in duality which is surfacing: on the one hand my duty of care for him feels undiminished, on the other hand his compulsion to establish his independence from me increases by the day. Part of his imperative to see my pastoral role come to an end manifests itself in him displaying, especially in front of his massive, that I have no authority over him whatsoever. I.e., he dissin' me.

He dissed me so bad this one Friday night during some five-a-side (that I kindly arrange for him and the massive) that he brought out my inner child and I forgot to take him to the match the following morning. It was not easy to pass by his street and not remember to pick him up (it hurt me as much as it hurt him, etc) but something had to be done. It was the Saturday before Christmas, an un-glitzy fixture away at Wimbledon, but one he'd been looking forward to in order to witness for himself how few people would be there. The Wimbledon fans have demonstrated to their custodians – who are moving their business to a shopping centre in Milton Keynes – that they have no authority over them either, by leaving to form their own club. There were about 1,000 supporters in the ground in total, mostly ours. It was a curious experience. Like watching televised Dutch football in the middle of the night, there was no atmosphere and far too much echo. This absence of atmosphere threw the game into a sharper light and as the match developed it became clear to me that a normal crowd at a first-team match distracts you from the play. You could hear all the player shouts, which added a strange dimension. Though watching football is a visual experience, it's highly aural too, but it's *us* who are supposed to supply the sound effects, not the players. The Germans have a word, *unheimlich*, which literally translated means un-homely, but which implies more than that – eeriness, hauntedness. To observe a competive game played in these conditions, the few hundred remaining Wimbledon fans banging the seats in front of them to give themselves voice – to rage against the dying of the light, to repudiate Lacan's silence – felt to me somewhat *unheimlich*, and the absence of my son only added to the sensation of wrongness.

Sitting in the cold gloom of West Norwood I could exonerate myself for indulging my inner child by saying I spared him from an entirely unremarkable 1–1 draw, the most entertaining aspect of which was that twenty or so of our supporters were to be seen eating their pies and smoking their fags dressed as Santa. But I felt un-exonerated and shoddy, that really all I was doing was adding hostility to our relationship. He's a true supporter, thoroughly involved in the narrative of the season. The compulsion of the true supporter is never to miss a game that doesn't have to be missed. (It is *not* to carry a Pikey little card saying 'True Supporter' on it. These didn't apply yet: the processing of applications.)

I felt I had handed down an extremely harsh punishment.

But I *had* been very badly dissed. Something really *did* have to be done.

I sold Jack's ticket cheap outside the ground (touts were conspicuous by their absence). The cheeky-faced boy on behalf of whom the purchase was made asked me how come I had it spare. I used shorthand: My lad's been grounded, I said.

Wow, the boy replied, That's harsh! I mean, my mum grounds me, but she'd *never* really carry it out for a Stoke match.

This pronouncement compounded my pre-existing mood of miserableness, which was quite distinct from the general melancholy created by conditions inside the stadium and the entertainment on offer. I contemplated the cheeky-faced boy's words for some time. Many mums and dads in Norwich know less than Homer Simpson about disciplining their children, hence an over-representation of spoilt brats out here on the Eastside. I had thought that this crisis of parenting was a disability confined to the dithering middle classes. I didn't know that such weakness could be found in Stoke too. And applied to my motherlode, I was minded to regard it as a progressive and enlightened approach. To draw a conclusion from this meant I had no choice but to regard myself as a dinosaur dad who probably had hairs growing out of his nose. Jack caught up with me some hours later on the mobile as I was driving back up the motorway: to assist the healing process between us I gave him a right bollocking for making me feel this way.

Tis the season to ship points and become mired in the relegation zone

The festive period and its aftermath with the traditional fixture pile-up can usually be relied upon to deliver nought points from a possible nine, a defender with a broken foot, and a goalie out for the remainder of the 'campaign' with a torn shoulder. This year is different. True, we lost 4–2 away at Bradford on Boxing Day: to have travelled to Yorkshire in a post-turkey haze to witness this would have found me in deep domestic mither. I went to Carrow Road instead hoping for a Norwich win as they were playing our relegation-rivals, bottom placed Brighton. Prior to this Norwich had lost one League game at home all season. It was odds-on Brighton would buck this trend simply to piss me off for being there; they came out 1–0 victors (1–0 is only ever a signifier of enjoyment if it's a win for your own team, otherwise it's more frequently known as 'a crap match'). But on the Saturday between Christmas and New Year, in the reverse of the opening-day fixture, we triumphed by scoring a last minute winner in a 3–2 thriller against our fellow dunces from Sheffield Wednesday. Our first win for *sixteen games*. And on New Year's Day we beat Preston North End, which was what I suspected would happen, because the very first thing I'd seen at the dawn of 2003 was a hogmanay television show on which Tom Jones was singing, of all things, 'Delilah'. It's not unusual to see Jones on the small screen, it *is* unusual to see him perform 'Delilah', a number from which he tends to distance himself since becoming a hip-hop *artiste*. I'd taken it to be a very good omen. And so it turned out to be. *Two wins in a row*! I was in no condition to deal with this, I simply didn't know how to feel. This glimpse of how life could be if you were the follower of a successful club had me reeling. How do people cope? You leave a game, you've won, you're happy. It's candyfloss with a toffee apple on the side. What about the anguish, pain and despair? What about the depression? Where is the meaning? And what is the point?

The situation was compounded by us *not* being knocked out of the FA Cup by Wigan Athletic, *nor* by AFC Bournemouth in the following tie either. AFC, I ask you, do they think Bournemouth's in Milan or something? Overcoming the AFCs put us into the fifth round, a mere three games from the final, for the first time since 1987, or to put it another way, since before Jack was born. Crazy days.

The outlook at the end of January filled us with anticipation. We jumped for joy as our reward for cup progress was Chelsea at home (we jumped for the glamour-factor; the outcome-factor was something to sit down and not think about). And the next League game was one we'd been anticipating for a good long time because it put me in the happy position of having a two-and-a-half-minute walk rather than a 200-mile drive to the ground, and it put Jack in the happy position of hanging round Norwich city centre pre-match wearing his colours and looking hard.

Every match is a big match for someone #2

There are times when it all comes together. This one began with a lengthy period of speculation on the prospects of a postponement and took into account awkward and protracted last-minute reconfigurations of plans for friends and family journeying from the Midlands. The travel problems created knock-on worries for me: the pre-match build-up was notable for painful whereabouts-of-tickets psychodramas due to road chaos – for the first time all season I was not carrying them myself. This will never happen again. From Ollie-the-dog's point of view (a lurcher rescue pup who had recently joined us) the pre-weekend period became associated with the trauma of far too many freezing cold walks round the ground to conduct pitch inspections. It may have been that an immediate return to the dog's home would have been his suggestion, if only dogs could talk (and I had yet to inform him which team he supported).

In short, there had been snow.

I was keen for us to play Norwich at this point, we were in our best (our only) mini-run since Pulis took over, and a cancellation due to weather could find us arriving for the rearranged fixture in a more typical patch of form. In reality, the undersoil heating at Carrow Road meant that the game was always going to take place, but I was unable to wholly believe this. I spent the morning sliding about in a high state of agitation. On a normal Saturday I have a full-time preoccupation; it was on this day that the true distraction-value and nerve-settling quality of the driving really came home. Still, as kick-off approached and family showed up and we assembled outside the Clarence Harbour public house and I caught sight of the tickets and a pint of iced-over Guinness, I was able to find a few moments of internal peace, here, with my tribe, in my home.

It took thirty-five seconds for our posse of East Anglian Exiles, associated hangers-on and thrill seekers to walk from the pub to the away enclosure. It took Norwich twice as long to score their first goal. At this, the finger that Jack had been displaying to his mates in the home end, who were close enough to see the digit in question, was returned with all the glee that you'd expect, plus the sign-of-the-wanker and, in addition, the gesture of the dickhead. For fuck's fucking sake. It took them one whole minute longer to score than when we last played here six years ago. That was the occasion of Jack laughing at me; this time I found myself employing emergency parental techniques involving shoring-up of spirits. Less than half an hour later we were two down. The second goal was a solar system offside and the linesman – who had been nowhere near the play, otherwise he may possibly have flagged this fact, though I doubt it, had a snowball hurled at him for his disgraceful ineptitude. I was enormously impressed: snow had been completely cleared from the ground (Health & Safety); we had in our midst a prodigy who had the foresight to secrete such an item through the turnstiles and to keep it cold. Maybe he'd stored it in a

Thermos? The stewards moved about in a purposeful manner looking for the culprit. Is snowball-throwing an arrestable offence, then? In the case of Stoke supporters in a football stadium the answer is almost certainly Yes, a situation that could only be exacerbated by Norwich being a location of the type where snowballing is on a list of banned playground activities. Hard to believe, but true. The missile flew narrowly wide of its target anyway – surely there can't be charges to answer for *that*?

There should certainly be charges to answer for our 'defending'. If you play like fucking schoolboys you get fucking dicked, as I heard one bloke comment to another in the half-time bogs. We remained 2–0 down at the interval, though it could easily have been worse. My morale was at rock bottom and Jack's was underneath it. Even the news that Sunderland[25] were 0–3 down at home to Charlton and that all three goals had been scored by their own players against themselves was of scant compensation. The prospect Jack and I were looking at was of being on the receiving end of merciless piss-taking (I'm gonna get slaughtered, as he put it) for the next few days, weeks, months, possibly even years to come. A nightmare, a daymare, the Honest sort of mare that trails the field a mile back and loses a tenner for you. Any sort of mare you've got. Fucking Stoke.

---

25 They had barely won a match since the Quitter's defection, they were a certainty for relegation (hahahahahahahahah). Provided we could stay up ourselves, we would be able to welcome the jug-eared git back to the Brit next year (yesyesyesyesyes yesyes).

Carrow Road was the final destination to which you could travel without the need to be a True Supporter. Perhaps because of this some fans were making their last stand: given the adverse weather and the distance involved, our following was more than decent in number. And suddenly, as the second half began, in much more than decent voice too. Some kind of snow madness took over and our singing worked itself to a crescendo. We ran through the entire repertoire, including full verse and chorus of the cup song that the team recorded in '72 – 'We'll be With You' (every step along the way) – which is in the vein of the England squad's 1970 groove 'Back Home' and doesn't often get the twelve-inch outing. It was stirring stuff, and I felt proud of us, to be giving it this at 2–0 down. In fact, it was so stirring that the team felt ashamed of themselves and atoned by producing a goal, a solid header scored by our other remaining first-choice Icelandic player, Brynjar Gunnarsson. Brynjar had been a star in the Second Division, but the step up to the First had exposed the limitations of his imagination and ability. It would be kindest to him to say he'd been having a very average year. I have noticed that he tends to lift his game when it's particularly cold – fortunately he'd arrived in Norwich to find weather conditions that suited him. The cross for his goal was provided by the damaged-swan Hoekstra who had decided that the second half at Carrow Road was the arena in which he was going to give his finest display of the season. When this happens, he's the best player on any First Division pitch by a distance.

We were back in it, and Jack felt confident enough to regesticulate at his mates who had turned sullen and were refusing either eye or finger contact. We were more than back in it, we were suddenly in charge. The day had begun, however, with Norwich in the top six and us in the bottom three. A home side that goes two up under those starting conditions will win. Still, I felt oddly sanguine. Suddenly the tide had turned and we were acquitting ourselves as well as we had all season. Though the team were losing, they were not actively embarrassing me, and that was almost enough. Take Thommo, for instance, our right back who is useless with his head in the specific sense that he is devoid of a brain. He clattered one of their players on the half-way line (his outstanding feature is his clumsiness). Normally he'd follow this up by threatening the bloke while he was still on the deck thus ensuring he'd get himself sent off. I almost admire him for this; in these days of the anodyne football robot he's the nearest we've got to a character. In a change to his predictable routine, Thommo went in for the novel technique of presenting imaginary stud marks down his thigh to the ref, as if it were the *other* player who was at fault, thereby only receiving a booking. I regarded this as real progress: could it possibly be the case that this nincompoop was coming to the realization that we play better with eleven men on the pitch than we do with ten? (Well, no worse, anyway.) His antics woke the home fans up, which had the effect of lifting his game. He fired on down the channel like an old-style wing-back, adding to our threat. Jack hunkered low in concentration beside me, pensive, but in an improved condition as a consequence of the one recovered goal. The sun dropped away in the west. For a moment I nearly felt happy.

Steve Banks, a goalkeeper, had joined us on loan to take over from Cutler. Cutler's psyche had taken too much of a battering from the constant defeats, and he was in need of rest, repair and TLC. Banks was a decent replacement with a comforting and resonant name on the back of his shirt; he had kept us in this match with an instinctive point-blank stop early in the second half – it was this moment that had unsettled Norwich. Stoke pushed on in waves; Norwich faltered. Lee Mills was another loanee, a journeyman forward who had been brought in only a couple of weeks earlier in yet another attempt to resolve the striker-crisis. We'd seen him for fifteen minutes in the previous game and he had looked overweight, snail-like, and had the turning circle of a double-decker bus. Honest? He looked as truthful as they come. He was carrying a black (and white) mark anyway so far as we were concerned: though he had arrived directly from Coventry (who are absolute crap) he had played a large part of his career for The Fail, who are obviously a good deal worse. Unacceptable.

Mills came on for the final half-hour and, in spite of his previous record, performed well. In the eighty-sixth minute he received the ball from the third loanee[26] of the day, Frazer Richardson. I could not warm to Richardson as he was temporarily occupying Bjarni's position and he was not Bjarni. If Pulis wanted to convince me beyond doubt that he was a

---

26 Team on the tic, we're just a team on the never never . . .

second-rate two-bob manager with no love of life, nothing would do it as quickly, efficiently and persuasively as dropping BG. However: Mills received a decent pass from the un-Bjarni and belied all that we'd seen from him the week before by turning on a sixpence to lash a shot from well outside the area which hit the top corner of the net like a rocket. The stadium stopped into quiet. The Norwich fans could not believe it. It came from nowhere. We could not believe it either, for the same reason plus one: it came from less than nowhere, this wonder-goal was ex-Vale stock. (!) The Mental that broke the silence was unsurpassed.

By the full-time whistle, Jack's mates had taken their sullenness to its logical conclusion and had disappeared completely. *Whatever*: it wouldn't put them out of reach of some txt sledging. He was delirious, and so was I, and so were the lot of us as we danced out through the gates cheering all the more as the news from the other bottom clubs flashed on the scoreboard – a full house of defeats. With the benefit of an easy departure from the away paddock, we found ourselves in the position of being able to pelt the home support with snowballs over the side of the Barclay End. The Canary boys found themselves wanting – no supplies of retaliatory material. Like ducks being shot at a funfair, a gang of fluorescent-orange stewards foolishly tried to deflect the barrage. In this ludicrous scene I found the true happiness I had come near to feeling earlier in the match: not only had we won the game by snatching a draw from the jaws of defeat with a quite stunning fluke goal, we were now thrashing them out of sight in the unopposed snowballing. Could a day be more perfect?

The bare statistics of the two big matches: three goals and two points apiece. All square. Finally Jack had a Monday morning to look forward to. The result had the effect of turfing Norwich out of the top six *for the first time since the season began*. We were elevated out of the relegation slots, from third-from-bottom to fourth-from-bottom, for the first time since early November, for the first time since our home defeat by Grimsby. It was February 1st: guess who we just exchanged places with. And guess where we play next.

I wash my hands of them

As if travelling to the Cleethorpes Riviera for a massive, massive relegation six-pointer was not enough to look forward to on its own, this was the first outing for the True Supporter to enjoy. I don't like to bang on, but it's worth emphasising that the fixture which was, to date, the most important of the season in terms of maintaining First Division status was to be the test case for this scheme. A big loud support might not go amiss, no? It's also worth mentioning that, easy though it may be to mock Grimsby simply because of its name, Blundell Park is without doubt the third (after the Bescot and Layer Road) bleakest dump in football, and is no great prospect for a day out even without the imposition of restrictions and the implication carried therein: that we followers are nothing but an inconvenient mob of knuckle-scraping troglodytes. It is my duty to report that with a sad and sorry shortfall in the business of Prominentism, the fighting went on elsewhere.

For a start, Tony Pulis had a scrap with the Grimsby assistant manager.

Post-Norwich, Thommo had reverted to type and in the aftermath of a characteristic incident the Grimsby assistant manager was encouraging the ref to send him off. Cutler, rested goalkeeper turned peacekeeper, sprang from the bench to remove Pulis from the Grimsby assistant manager's neck. On the pitch, in a Battle of the Giants, Bjarni (who was only on as sub anyway) and James O'Connor squared up to each other to argue the toss over who was having the worst match. A Bjarni-hater amongst us who clearly gave this award to Gudjonsson was rounded on. *Who the fuck, who the fuck, who the fucking hell are you?* we chanted at him. He required a mini police-cordon to see him out of the ground. In the absence of alternatives, and in the light of events, we fought amongst ourselves. Inspired.

It was becoming our leitmotif to concede in the first minute. It was becoming traditional to follow this up by shipping another goal twenty minutes later. The team stuck to these rituals: why tamper with a losing formula? During the preceding week it had been reported that the Icelandic contingent had been celebrating their Thorri (winter) feast. Various gastro-treats were on the menu, puffin flippers and sour rams' testicles amongst them. I'd rather have been eating those rolled up raw in a cold oatcake than watching us play the sort of football that would make a dog vomit. *Sorglegur* is an Icelandic word for pathetic. We were two down and playing as sorglegurically as it is possible to play. In a popular Stoke expression that I heard many times that day, as well as on many other occasions, we were utter garbage.

With a droll delivery, Jack raised a specific: How much does this cost, Dad?

Seventeen quid for my ticket, thirteen for yours, thirty-odd for petrol. Programme, chips, whathaveyou, about seventy quid, I replied.

He looked at me.

I looked at him.

You could pick up a Burberry jacket for that in the sales, and we both knew it. But I was encouraged by his question. Normally Jack is seethingly upset in the face of a display of this type. I have seen tears of rage in his eyes. I noted in this more-or-less ironic enquiry the first sign of an oblique resignation which, if carefully nurtured, can develop into full-blown stoicism.[27] Full-blown stoicism is an essential requirement to soldiering on, it can help in life in general as well as in Stoke-watching and cannot be acquired by following Man United.

There's a line in the Beth Orton song, 'Pass in Time',[28] which

---

27 Stolcism is the word which comes directly before 'stoke' in the New Oxford Dictionary of English.

28 Track 5 on the album *Central Reservation*. A wonder song of hope in the face of loss. (The title is nothing to do with James O'Connor's ability to locate one of his colleagues when releasing the ball.)

goes *All your doubts become your own beliefs*. This was happening in front of our eyes. Peter Handyside, our 'captain' (I had never seen him demonstrate authority; he has no discernible personality) was returning to his old club for the first time. He put in a shaky, nervous, timid, docile and messy display entirely lacking in conviction. Where he flunked in his duty of leadership, the team followed. The pre-Christmas culture of failure was re-establishing itself. We could only compete – in a manner that would adequately define the word – against sides placed higher than us. In a contest against better players we were able to raise our game. Left to find our own level against equivalents we were unable to deliver a response. Equivalents: Iceland has a population the equivalent of Stoke. Though they had once been rich enough to buy our club, the Icelandics were beginning to betray a truth: that their ability to run it was slightly unequivalent to ours, that they were even *less* adept at it than we are ourselves.

2–0 was the final score. Once more we had been comprehensively outplayed and outfought by Grimsby. *Brjóstumkennanlegur* is another Icelandic word. We were a disgrace, we were brjóstumkennanlegur. Brjóstumkennanlegur also means pathetic.

Jack and I wasted very little breath on post-match debriefing on the drive back and even less about our prospects against Chelsea next week. We kept our spirits buoyed by addressing matters outside football. The boy's stoic streak was up and running.

Back home I lay on the floor half-watching *Match of the Day* (it may be on ITV and be called *The Premiership*, but I can only think of Saturday night highlights as *MotD* and can only hope that one day it will return and be a proper programme once again). I rubbed my neck, which ached from driving.

Are you all right, Trezza asked.

My own supplies of indifference in the face of unceasing adversity were low.

I will be happy when the season ends and I do not have to do this any more, I replied.

Not far off a football genius

We listened to an interview on Radio Stoke as we crawled through the traffic for the cup tie. Our manager said that having Chelsea in town would provide the good people of the Potteries with the opportunity to watch some quality players. He also said he had not talked about Chelsea too much to our team as he did not want to frighten them. There was much more in the same vein, none of which was easy on the ear either in the sense of the words themselves or in the nasal Welsh/West Country accent in which they were delivered. If it was clear enough by now that Pulis was short on charm and charisma, that he was unintelligent enough to go talking rubbish of this sort in public in this way was unexpected and unpleasant news. Like his ex-chairman at Gills, I was beginning to think I would be much happier when he was out of my life.

His efforts to bond with the Stoke public had not gone beyond irritatingly repeating his mantra that Stoke City is a 'triffic' and 'proper' club (really?). Other than that, his encounters with the local press and radio tended to centre on ill-disguised comments concerning the limitations of his team. If this was his way of trying to get money out of the board (which is surely the best interpretation) then it was an uncouth method of going about it and could send out only one message to the squad. Pulis's team building within this group was clearly non-existent: you could see at a glance that they were barely playing for each other, and certainly not for their manager. Ben Keane had been bitten by the bug and was once more back in the Midlands for a football match, and once more he was shaking his head in a manner that was fast becoming a tradition. Familiarization with the fundamental aspects of sports psychology would not go amiss for Mr Pulis, Ben suggested. I couldn't help but agree. And he could do worse than acquainting himself with the basic tenets of media-handling while he was at it. I could only second that too. 'The Boys Are Back In Town' went on earlier than is customary, to drown the fucker out.

The full-house signs were up at the Britannia for the first time since Jack's conversion to Stoke three years earlier. Deprived of our preferred seats in the new Boothen End, we were forced into the East Stand. Nine thousand of us had bothered to attend the first cup match against Wigan Athletic. There were 26,500 here today. Jack was driven to comment on this situation: Glory-hunting knobs. Well, Mr Chairman, what about it? There will be sell-outs if there are – as your manager has identified – some quality players on view. We lost 2–0 as usual, which a great many people seemed to think entitled us to hold our heads up and be proud. My mind boggled. This was Chelsea we were talking about, not Real Madrid – elsewhere in the same competition Crystal Palace of the First Division had beaten Liverpool of the Premiership. It *can* happen; it *does* happen. The programme (£3 rather than the usual £2.50 – not to mention hiking up the price of the extras too, Mr Chairman) featured Alan Hudson as cover model. There was a certain appropriateness in being reminded of the louche maestro: nostalgia – it's the natural rest home for the terminally unambitious.

In the post-match interview Pulis was asked how (now we'd got the cup business out of the way for the next fifteen years) he saw the prospects of remaining in the First Division. He wasn't too sure we could do it with the current personnel.

I gave in. Even if this was patently obviously the case, does a triffic manager of a proper club say it in public? How does such a comment impinge on a team whose morale is already in intensive care? Can you imagine Sir Alex Ferguson coming up with such defeatist clap-trap even after a defeat? No way, when Man United lose it's the referee, it's the other officials and it's the wrong colour shirts that are to blame. And that's the way it should be.

Are we Vale in disguise?

Following their pride-inducing cup display against Chelsea, life returned to normal for Stoke. Back in the League the situation looked ominous when, at the City Ground, Nottingham, they failed to concede a goal in the first minute. The 800-weak following (a thousand or two down on the normal figure) fell silent as they settled expectantly into the Bridgford Lower Stand and looked to a possible future: Meadow Lane, home of Second Division Notts County was clearly in view. Occasionally the Stoke crowd glanced up from the action to identify who, from amongst the impeccably behaved Forest support perched above them in the Bridgford Upper, was spitting.

Four quick goals in twenty short excruciating minutes silenced the following even further. Only the tinkle of coins being chucked from the Upper Bridgford punctured the hopeless inertia. The young colt who scored all four goals, Marlon Harewood, deserves special mention for being a magnificent striker and not at all the sort of player on whom Stoke would waste good money.[29] An Icelandic defender was

---

29 Of course, one man's poison is another man's meat and every cloud has a silver lining. We do provide a service in supplying happier statistics for the clubs we play than we do for ourselves. Harewood's fine effort was the first time a Forest player had scored four in one match in fourteen seasons.

sent off. The 800 made the sound of the boo at the interval as goalkeeper Banks shook his head and looked sad.

H/T Forest . . . 4 City . . . 0

Finally finding their voice as things picked up in the second period, the diehard true-supporting crew rocked the house: *Shall we sing a song for you?* they chorused at a home support who were in carnival mood. A jaunty *We're shit and we know we are* was followed by several rousing renditions of *5–4 . . . we're gonna win 5–4; 6–5 . . . we're gonna win 6–5*, and finally *7–6 . . . we're gonna win 7–6*. The physical gesture of mirth that is traditionally demonstrated to opponents who put the ball high and wide of the target – the arms-wide *aaarrrggghhh* – was generously displayed to Stoke's *own* players by Stoke's own fans. As Forest took their boot off the gas and City managed to string three passes together you could just see the next one coming: *Brazil, it's just like watching Brazil*. Yet even in the midst of all this the 800 found time to chorus, in a counterpoint to the ironic despair, and as an example to the directors, players and manager of SCFC (we thank you for your continuing support), a full, committed (look it up), and forlorn 'Delilah'.

As the match petered out and Stoke City slid to the bottom of the table, as all around hopes lay dead and dying, the final unedifying question, as title of this passage, could clearly be heard.

Stoke Holding had spent some energy over the past weeks trying to purchase Port Vale, who had gone into administration. Steady on now comrades, if you can't run one football club, what makes you think you can run two?

F/T Nottingham Forest . . . 6 (six) Stoke City . . . 0[30]

Old Stokie

Towards the end of Gudjon's tenure, I found myself bidding in an internet auction for a crush barrier (it can happen) which had been part of the fixtures and fittings of the old Boothen End at the old Victoria ground. Finishing up the winner as the virtual hammer went down, I travelled to Stoke to pick up the magnificent item. I'd like to say I tied this journey in with a match, but actually I went specifically to pick up the barrier. Here I met its custodian, a legendary figure around *The Oatcake* messageboard, a man who, though he has a real name, is widely know by his online alter-ego, Old Stokie. Being both technologically backward and naturally suspicious of online chat forums, I was something of a late arrival at the messageboard. For a time I looked in without contributing, watching in silent fascination as Old Stokie conversed with TEL2U, plymptonpotter and a host of others, including even his own boy (who, in homage to the Icelandic connection, goes under the moniker Old Stokiesson). Most of the chatter was about football but some of it was about any

---

30 And this was Forest's biggest win for eight years.

other topic you'd care to name. Debates were conducted in an informed, searching and humorous spirit, with occasional forays into bonkers-ness and outbreaks of bad temper. My favourite time to look in was late at night, when I tend to be at my computer.

Of all the cyberfans whose opinions I began to know, Old Stokie was a favourite, both for his energy and dedication, his specialized brand of madness, and his instinct to discursiveness. Not to mention his alarming output. If I could produce a quarter of his daily output I'd write three times the amount that I actually do. Each message has a headline, for example <u>Thommo – Clinically Insane???</u> or <u>Saturday is a MUST MUST WIN game NOW!!!</u> These headlines develop into 'threads' which grow in length as more cyberfans join in, and then fall away and 'drop off the board' as new topics take over. Sometimes participants are rebuked in one thread for contradicting something they said in another. Normally they will deny this and put it down to misinterpretation, moronicity and fçükwittedness (spellings have to be customized to get through a bad language-filter) in the thread-reader. And so on. All teams have these fanzine boards. Ours are amongst the most heavily-trafficked in all Leagues in England and Scotland. Here can be identified another distinguishing characteristic of Stokies: verbalists, aficionados of good nogger[31] natter. I always

---

31 Archaic Stoke term for football. Usage: Comin' out for a game of nogger? Nah, conner be bothered.

imagine a great deal of this online activity taking place from workplace computers – the daytime is busier than the night – with fans abusing their terms of employment. We are natural insubordinates too. Perhaps that might be something to be proud of. (Or not. We are not insubordinate enough, otherwise we'd have fçüked off the board, the useless councillors, the crappy business sharks, et al., long ago. We need a shake-up and a thorough re-examination of ourselves as a matter of urgency. Actually, we need to stop talking and to fçüking do something.)

One night OS headed a message to the effect that he'd be away for some time. The body of the message informed us that his wife had died. I called Trezza over. Look, I said. Trezza mocks me for the life I waste on *The Oatcake*, but I had mentioned Old Stokie to her often enough for us both to shed a tear. A long and impressive list of condolences built up.

Back then I had not given myself a user name. By the time I met OS to pick up the magnificent crush barrier, he knew me as 'winger'. He turned out to be as engaging in person as he was online, and a friendship of the type that modern football is able to nurture began: public exchanges on the messageboard acknowledging that we each knew of the other in real life developed into rude sledgings and so on. And on the side we exchanged occasional emails as well as actual postcards and items of interest. Sometimes I'd even slip into Delilah's Bar for a quick commiseratory post-match lime and soda with him. At the Forest game for the first time, and by chance, we sat together. OS had Old Stokiesson, who is a few years younger than me, alongside him, and I had Jack. We sat in seats at a level-change so we had a low wall before us upon which we leant, chins in hands. As the goals rained in we talked for the first time at any length, OS and I. Face to face, that is. He'd found out about my work, and had read some of my stuff and I appreciated his interest and his kind words and in the shallow writerly way I liked him all the more for it. In addition to his kind words, I admired his attire – he wears a classic sheepskin commentator's coat and a hat to match. He is slight inside the coat, with a permanent twinkle in his eye under the hat. As the scoreline grew ever worse we deflected ourselves from feeling too injured by what our team weren't doing for us out on the pitch by talking away about more or less anything other than the main subject. By the finish we could have been watching 'One Man and his Dog'. I'm not sitting next to you again, he said as we took our leave, You're a bad luck charm. Speak for yourself, I replied.

As we drove away, on the back of the 6–0 stuffing, the txts that Jack was receiving were being supplemented by actual calls (his ring-tone plays 'Delilah', like all Stokies' phones; this provokes a mass-reach for the mobile when one goes off at the match) enquiring about how he enjoyed his afternoon. His responses were superb:

Yes, can I help you?

Hmm, why exactly are you on the phone? I can't seem to understand the reason for your call.

Isn't there something important you should be doing, rather than wasting your credit?

He also appeared happy within himself to the extent of seeming positively beatific. Viewing him from my usual sidelong position, my suspicions were aroused that Stoke-following might be elevating itself into the it's-so-bad-it's-good category. I wasn't sure I could condone that – such an attitude should be reserved for activities like watching *Pop Idol* and playing 'HotorNot' on the net. He had made little comment during the game. This was revealing in itself and I could tell from aspects of his body language that he had enjoyed the experience of sharing the match in the company of a legend. I was able to imagine an alternative and more palatable diagnosis to account for his mood: that it was just a straightforward case of a good student observing and absorbing OS's masterclass in stoicism.

The followers' fear of the goalless draw

Dry sex may be less rewarding than a game in which the pill never hits the back of the net, but not much else in voluntary human activity provides as little pleasure commensurate to the effort invested. We put together three un-orgasmic blinders in a row: away to Ipswich, home to Sheffield United, and away to Wolverhampton Wanderers. In the context of our League position – we'd semi-recovered from the Forest trauma with nervous yet vital home wins against Walsall and fellow relegation candidates Brighton,[32] but we remained in the bottom three – each point had to be viewed with positivity, as each point was secured against sides with Premiership Aspirations. But watching on from the stands you had to ask whether the human life you were losing in terms of time, and the money you were getting rid of in terms of pounds, could in any way be justified. They were matches of unsurpassed tedium, as if all concerned were on their honour to play vow-of-poverty football of the lowest conceivable specification. Over the course of four-and-a-half hours plus stoppage time Stoke failed to force a goalkeeper into satisfying his job description even *once*. It should not, therefore, have been difficult for the oppositions to look good. But to their collective shame it was beyond the scope of those thirty-plus different outfield players from three other teams to muster between the lot of them anything more than the token lackadaisical shot that travelled even vaguely in the direction of the target. We cleared one off the line at Molineux[33] and for a

32 The season had reached the point where we were tracking this team's results, alongside Sheffield Wednesday's and Grimsby's, as a matter of course. Only one from this gang of four could escape the drop.

33 Like Preston North End, Wolves are another club who have redeveloped their home on its existing site rather than assemble a collection of industrial warehouses on a wind-blasted hill. Molineux is a decent stadium to visit, but Wolves-following must come second only to Stoke-following in terms of misery-generation. They are better than we are, but not by much, and have spent £60 million of Sir Jack Hayward's fortune to achieve this hopeless condition. You can imagine our grocers sitting shaking their heads at such a dreadful waste of money as they flick through the pages of their jet-ski catalogues. Wolves did finally achieve promotion to the Premiership this season though, at the fifteenth time of asking. (Actually, then, they

second my pulse-rate quickened. But that was *it*. Even taking into account the increasingly hazardous financial circumstances into which football was descending[34] those thirty-plus players would be handsomely rewarded for this tripe; they would pocket ten times an average weekly wage each easily. The value-for-money factor here is impossible to locate.

We were, though, making it awkward for them: Pulis was becoming pragmatic in the extreme – he was acquiring a new big lump of a defender on a loan deal as often as he possibly could, playing five at the back and four across the middle and abandoning the one desolate striker to a solitary life up front in the hope that the ball might bounce from his head at an unlikely angle and chance its way into the net. While we were horrible to watch and were never going to score in a million years, at the same time we were becoming difficult to break down. If you want entertainment, go and watch clowns. The only possible reason for attending football matches of this sort is to heighten the context for witnessing exceptional doings in the lives of players such as:

---

are much better than us.) And what did Sir Jack say about this? He said he did it for the fans, the rightful owners of the club. Madness, eh?

34 Clubs were going into administration, often voluntarily, as a matter of routine, as a device for restructuring their entire financial footing. Particularly ill-affected were teams who'd recently dropped from the Premiership, whose players were still on Premiership money, i.e. anything from £10,000 to £30,000 a week plus bonuses. Ipswich, who I've earlier cited as a well-run outfit, became an unexpected example of this syndrome.

Peter Hoekstra

On the trip to Vicarage road, the Watford stadium which rests atop a bank of allotments in metroland, I asked Jack a question – a variation of 'you don't have to do it for me'.

Do you still *like* doing this?

Though I recognized that his dedication to the season was beyond question, I found it hard to believe that he could possibly be getting anything out of it any more and that it wasn't merely a sense of duty that was motivating him.

C'mon Dad, he said. This is *Stoke* we're talking about.

I felt suitably rebuked.

Though he enjoys the danger of night matches at Molineux (he knows a boy who knows a boy whose Norwich-supporting brother got bashed with a traffic cone by Wolves fans last season), and the kudos of belonging to a rough tribe outside of his own crew on the Eastside, I had not worked out that he was by now fully into the matrix. There is a dark admixture of something not unlike pleasure involved in Stoke-life. Our excursions are the crystallization of all-consuming maniac expectation that, actually, we enjoy, and which certainly provides a locus for flagging moments in conversation: Jack has a habit of calling me late at night for a grunt – speculation on the outcome of Saturday's game will always enliven our grunting.

It's when the anticipation becomes compounded by

wondrous events, when, incredibly, fulfilment is to be discovered at the journey's end, that the feelings thus provoked pass the bounds of plausible explanation. If a film were to be made of our jubilating crowd as the second of Peter Hoekstra's strikes went in on this day and titled, *Stoke City Fans Celebrate a Goal at Watford*, and if the film was subsequently played on a video loop in a white room it would walk the Turner Prize. Only in the communal death-pacts of American cults could you witness a greater number of simultaneous out-of-body experiences.

Hoekstra's damaged-swanlike running technique is a deliberate compensatory action to protect certain parts of his legs from further injury. Imagine this – *styling* your running to allow you to continue playing. It's much harder than it looks, football,[35] as it is, without having to consider how you travel over the ground to do it, an action which, for most of us, comes as naturally as our handwriting. Hoekstra is tall, almost gawky, and slightly ungainly to go with the studied running, but he can control the ball in a mesmerizing manner. He has appeared for the Dutch national team. So how is it that he is playing for us?

---

35 I sometimes reflect, when I'm criticizing a player, on how it would be if it were me down there. For a start I'd be puffing and panting and having a stitch after five minutes. And then there'd be this sort of thing: during a park game with the massive I dived for a header in the box. I mistimed my dive to the net effect that the ball went under my face, between head and ground, so that it scraped my nose before I landed on my stomach on top of it. Elegant it was not. Imagine the barracking I'd have to give me for that. (I always play to win though. There is *that* that distinguishes me from certain Stoke City line-ups.)

The leg injury which his swan-weave protects left him physically depleted and in search of employment. The rest of the story is something to do with Gudjon. Suffice it to say we don't often end up with rejects from Ajax and we aren't asking too many questions, though part of the answer will lie in the fact that Hookey (the inevitable re-namey) isn't always much of a game-reader.

During this match he had been making idiosyncratic, stylish, yet ineffective runs along the wing to deliver crosses to places where his teammates weren't. He'd been receiving criticism from some amongst us for being a Show Pony and for Showboating. Each of these clichéd expressions is attributable to Big Ron Atkinson. Overhearing parroted Ronisms is an inevitable lollipop of football-life early-doors. Hoekstra had atoned for his unacceptable flashiness by scoring from a penalty at the other end of the ground. This was the seventeenth away match we had attended and the first time we had seen us take a lead into the break. A break which was further vitalized by having a Page Three stunna in amongst us at the tea-stall, a girlfriend of one of Pulis's many many loanees.[36] My instinct was to be aloof from such celebrity spotting, but, you know, half-time, the allotments in view, 1–0 to us – even though I barely recognized her with her clothes on, her appearance nonetheless raised a smile, adding to the un-Stokeness of the interval, and our supporters celebrated by serenading her with a tender love song.

---

36 The same XI never started twice in the last dozen games.

Early into the second half, Hoekstra, with his back to goal and two defenders on him, received the ball outside the area. He half-turned and hit it. The arc it began to describe sent my attention to the goalkeeper's positioning. A few yards off his line. How could Hoekstra have seen that with his back to goal? He could not. One of the distinguishing characteristics of the player who is blessed with preternatural ability is that he holds a freeze-frame of the whereabouts of his colleagues and rivals for fractions of seconds, so that as he plays in real time he also accesses a time-lapse facility. I was perfectly positioned to see a consequence of this enigmatic talent, I was directly in line with the flight of the ball. The top-spin with which Hoekstra's left boot had laced it helped to loop it over, down and beyond the keeper as he desperately backtracked, but there remained two non-scoring possibilities:

1) it could strike the angle; or

2) it could land on the roof of the net.

I could see all this and think all this as the ball found its way into the absolute top corner having described the only possible parabola that would have allowed for such an outcome while clearing the still desperately backtracking keeper. It was an arrested moment that I will always be able to replay to myself. This is in the place where the out-of-body experience actually takes place – in the back of the mind.

2–0. Watford pull one back, the ref, as he is contractually required to, adds six minutes of stoppage time, but, on our seventeenth away journey of the season, we see us win for the first time. This is the nearest I can get to an explanation of the unreasonable dark pleasure: it's the enormous amount of mundanity we go through (another thing we're good at in Stoke – soaking it up) which makes the rewarding of the maniac anticipation so remarkable.

In his, *This is* Stoke *we're talking about* Jack gave me to understand that his comprehension of this state of affairs was complete. It's the routine awfulness of the performances combined with the iniquity of the officiating – and just because we're paranoid *doesn't* mean they're not out to get us – that furnishes elevated moments leading to intermittent triumphs with their profound value.

We drove home happy. We were third from bottom.

A boy's own life

And what does third from bottom mean? It means that the acquisition of points occupies our every thought.

By night I dream of saving them. They drop into my hands from the air like bubbles and burst upon my palms. By day Jack's calls are arriving at all times. He will txt at lunchbreak having picked up some on-loan information while abusing the facilities during double ICT. He is always on standby to discuss permutations of results in the other matches that affect us – to hypothesize upon how the points the others will pick up or drop can impinge on our lives. I can never retain all this information, but I can never forget the one outstanding fact, with which I wake every morning. The one outstanding fact is this: we are still down there. We are looking over our shoulder at the real possibility of an actual return to the Second Division. We are looking all the way down to the top of the Third, to see who will be promoted, who will humiliate us by requiring us to visit their wretched ground. Hartlepool United are certainties, which is fearful enough in itself, not to mention that Jack has an uncle there – I have a brother-in-law there – who will make the most of our misfortune, as I would to him were the positions reversible.

We find ourselves hooked by televised games that do not feature our bad selves.

Why are you cheering for Nottingham Forest? asks Trezza.

Because they're playing Grimsby (who, God only knows how, are leading 2–1).

'Of course; stupid of me.'

Another night, another nailbiter:

'Why are you cheering for who the fucking hell are Reading? Don't tell me – because they're playing Brighton?'

She's got the hang of it, and, God only knows how, but once more a fellow drop candidate is 2–1 up against a top-six side. *What* is going on? It's a plot. They are all in it together, they must be, it's the only explanation. They hate us, they hate our 'Delilah', they can't abide it that we are a hundred times better supporters than they are even in spite of the team we follow, and they are collaborating to see us go back down.

At our five-a-sides, I mention my conspiracy theory to Jack's massive. They respond with their *Yeah, right*s, and their *Whatever*s.

As far as this season is concerned, the massive have given up on Norwich City, who insist on contriving losses or draws from matches they might win, not least the points they conceded to us, as it is our duty to remind them, often. Norwich will clearly not make the play-offs. Norwich are shit. Norwich are bottlers. We are shit too, but in a different more laughable manner, and as the Canaries have nothing left to play for the attention of the posse has latched on to Stoke's battle to survive. The Hozzmeister, Milo, Watton, Luke, Lental, Woods, DJ Sammy, John Mosley: one by one each of these rudeboys has been over to the Midlands, to sample at first hand the Britannia experience. They are unimpressed, but in a good way. Jono, the most arch of them, has travelled *three* times, and is patently, at least partially, in so-bad-it's-good territory; he is spending money in the club shop on photos of our worst players. He is up to something. He will be assembling a gallery of naff-rubbishness on his bedroom wall, that is the sort of something he is up to. Jono's method of dealing with a world that is often difficult and alarming is to treat it with scorn, derision, and ridicule. He puts me in mind of Holden Caulfield in *The Catcher in the Rye*, a favourite book from my youth. (There is a racehorse called Catcher in the Rye. I will not back it; the title of a sacred text is no name for a horse.)

I have never spoken to Jono's parents, who also split up some few years ago. They live nearby, but I would not know them if I saw them in the street. I wonder what he tells them he is doing; I wonder whether they even know he is 200 miles from home watching poor-quality football matches in an ironic spirit. He could simply pass this off as 'Sleeping-over at Foster's dad's house.' It happens, it's a part of the way in which we parent now, collectively, by assumption, vaguely, on the ad hoc basis, occasionally losing track of them as they go off the block for a day or two. During the times when I don't know where Foster is or what he's up to, though, I feel sure he will not be travelling to Barnsley or Bury to watch football of diminished specification. There is enough of that in his life as it is.

Jono comes along for the night match v Rotherham. We are 1–0 up at the interval. This is not the first time Jono has seen such a thing. He is a lucky mascot.

Early into the second half I am sharing an old man moment with Graham Etherington (who does not miss a game except for the birds – he is a twitcher, though he says he is not, he says that he is a birder, and that birders are different to twitchers. There is a distinction here which I refuse to acknowledge; twitcher is the birdier word). The old man moment goes as follows: I am in Stoke, on a cold[37] night, I am home, I have my mini-massive with me – Jack, Jono, Graham and my mum. I am watching Honest Andy Cooke play to the very acme of his ability. Cookie is coming back from injury, and I am saying to Graham, I would love to see Cookie score. He works hard, he is a Stokie, he runs his legs off, he tries his heart out, he deserves a goal, bless his little cotton socks. Graham is nodding. He is not simply indulging me in the sentimental old man moment, he is

---

37 It's mid-April. It's always a good idea to take a coat if you're going to Stoke.

positively agreeing. He would love to see Cookie score too, as much as he would love to catch sight of the rare Houbara Bustard, not least because it would put us 2–0 up and make the three points look that much more secure.

I am in the mood for seeing a soul saved, like Holden in *The Catcher*. Holden imagines a scenario in which he is able to prevent children from falling over the edge as they play in the cliff-top field of rye, the only useful thing he can picture himself doing with his life. We all picture ourselves. Graham pictures himself there in '62 when the Houbara was last around. Me? In trying to make the sentences as well as I can, shaping the paragraphs from them, I imagine another person being prepared to read the result. The boys would like to – what? – succeed at something they are good at, same as anyone. *There's no success like failure*, Bob Dylan sang, *And failure's no success at all*. I recall this line often. It's in the back of my mind alongside sentences written by J. D. Salinger and Peter Hoekstra's goal, to be replayed whenever I want. Though my instinct is always to disagree with this lyric I cannot even begin an argument, beguiled as I am by the obviousness of its truth. I know this: I would die of boredom if I watched a team week-in week-out who won week-in week-out. There *is* no success without failure. This is why supporters of other teams hate Man United and their 'fans'. It is not that we envy them their success, it is that we despise them their ignorance of real life and its burdens.

Cookie's dreams and desires, Cookie's pictures of himself, are handicapped not only by his own limitations, but by the impossible weight of expectation that we confer upon him.

They must feel it, these footballers of limited merit. Each of them must sense from time to time that more is sought from them than they are capable of providing. They have to be prepared to fail; that is the price they pay for the acclaim they receive when it goes the other way. Whether or not they experienced the kind of parent who lives life by proxy, the inadequate you find at the school pitch-side yelling insanely at the ten-year-old, they will have seen it. They will know what goes on. We must not inflict this on our children, it is wrong. We must allow them to know that there is no success like failure. They will discover the other half of the line easily enough for themselves.

I have barely finished saying the old man words to Graham when Cookie receives a pass just inside the opposition half. He advances a pace or two. He looks to his right, he looks to his left, to see if he can rid himself of the alarming object at his feet: there is not a colleague in sight. He leathers the ball like thunder. He lets fly a piledriver that makes for the back of the net like a smart bomb, fizzing and looping over the astonished keeper from forty yards out as it tears down the middle of the goal. Up in the stands we cannot believe what we have seen, and we shake our heads in wonder. If he ever does that again, I will eat my trousers. I am so glad for him that he did it this once, though, that I have a tear in my eye, to match my mum's, who always cries when we score. Because here she is, with her grandson, who does not need to support Stoke City, the team she has always followed, but who *does* support them, and who even brings his friends along too, to add to the extended family that she is always building (her survival instinct: she lost her own parents very young, she had no one to yell insanely at her from the touchline). I restrain myself from shedding more of the same tears – unacceptable in front of Jack, and imagine what Jono would have to say about it – but I know how she feels.

As the team swamps Cookie in celebration and we swamp each other it is my belief that I have helped him score by wishing it on him. Now my old man moment is complete: I am away with the fairies, over the moon. Soon, at least, the season will be over.

The heroic goal, the second of the night, is the next-but-one since Hoekstra's at Watford. Two belters nearly in a row; you can't knock that. In the meantime we witnessed yet another scoreless extravaganza, this time at home to Gillingham, an exhibition of footballing grandeur that made the bore-athons against Ipswich, Sheffield United and Wolves look like Royal Variety Performances. Gillingham, and all those others, were the backdrops that heightened the context for Andrew Cooke's defining career highlight. At the Wolves bore-athon it was he who was the lonely desolate who spent his whole night with his back to goal, playing alone up front simply to hold the ball, to buy the midfield breathing space. You really do have to see it all to understand how the world works.

Thommo makes an outstanding contribution to an outstanding night as he manages to provoke a Rotherham player into headbutting him, thus earning a sending off. We do not lose 4–0 to Rotherham. Instead we win 2–0, the only time this season that we will record a victory by more than a single goal. The three points are ours. Six matches remain: there are eighteen more to play for.

Maybe it's possible that we *can* avoid the drop. Perhaps we are *not* beyond salvation.

It's a long-distance train pulling through the rain on the return from a night fixture. The boys help me through the miles, they remind me to keep it real with their inane ramblings as they coat the back seat of the car with crumbs and sticky stuff from their Liquorice Allsorts and chips and Red Bulls. I am a fiasco, habitat-wise, the only place I take pride in maintaining in a neat and tidy condition is the interior cabin area of my car. It is where I like to do some of my thinking, and I like to think in tidiness. Still, I accept their debris and the cleaning up it creates as the price I pay for the de-stressing service that the hum of their conversation provides. And I like to think I help them in return, by being unfunny in a fashion they can easily ridicule, by liking music they can revile, by wearing unsuitable clothing, by reconfirming them in their safe belief that adults are knobheads.

We talk football some more. We glance in the other direction in the League too. We discuss the likelihood of playing West Ham next season. We will certainly be visiting Sunderland, if we continue with our resistance. As far as the Premiership is concerned they are already doomed. Serve them right. Same goes for West Bromwich Albion. The third to fall will be culled from the Hammers, Leeds or Bolton. We'd prefer to make away days to any of these destinations than to Rushden & Diamonds, a team who enter our conversation as we make our way through Northamptonshire, the county of their home, the

Rose of the Shires, as it says on the sign. Rushden & Diamonds are on their way up from the Third Division along with Hartlepool. Jono holds to the idiosyncratic idea that Burnley are not a proper team and should not be in the same division as Norwich City. I hold to the entirely un-idiosyncratic idea that Rushden & Diamonds are the *less* glamorous club in Northamptonshire, which is saying something, and that I sincerely don't want to be paying them a visit them next year.

Rushden & Diamonds wouldn't be so far away, Eastside-wise. Rushden & Diamonds would be the new Colchester United. Rushden & Diamonds are the nightmare that puncture my dreams of points saved.

The mini League

The papers began publishing at-a-glance boxes like this:

Going down? Remaining fixtures

STOKE CITY		BRIGHTON		SHEFF WED		GRIMSBY	
19 April		**19 April**		**19 April**		**19 April**	
Wimbledon	H	Leicester	A	Grimsby	H	Sheffield Wed	A
21 April		**21 April**		**21 April**		**21 April**	
Coventry	A	Sheffield Wed	H	Brighton	A	Walsall	H
26 April		**26 April**		**26 April**		**26 April**	
Crystal Palace	A	Watford	H	Burnley	A	Reading	A
4 May		**4 May**		**4 May**		**4 May**	
Reading	H	Grimsby	A	Walsall	H	Brighton	H

	P	W	D	L	GD	Pts	FORM (most recent right)
Stoke	42	9	14	19	-26	41	W L W D D D W D W L
Brighton	42	10	10	22	-20	40	W L L W W L D D W L
Sheff Wed	42	8	14	20	-23	38	D L W D L D L D W W
Grimsby	42	9	10	23	-35	37	D L L D W W D L L L

to enable us all to see at the drop of a point who would be where and what awful happenings would be the consequence. The broadsheet papers ran stories about Brighton & Hove Albion. The tabloids ran stories about David Beckham's crop top. Brighton and Hove Albion are the team the broadsheets would like to see survive because the broadsheet journalists are southern nancy boys. There is not a single piece on Stoke City, because Stoke is a hole in the Midlands and the club has never knowingly cultivated a media contact and would not recognize a press release if I sent them one.

Still. Looking at the mini League box – we at least get a mention here – if you know anything about football, other than that Brighton is a nice place by the seaside with a club who deserve to stay up so you can have them as your second team (after Arsenal) for your weekends away in Sussex, you'd have to say we have the best looking run-in:

Wimbledon: nothing to play for.

Coventry: absolute crap.

Crystal Palace: deadly rivals of Brighton, bound to let us have at least a point.

Reading: all being well they'll be in the play-offs (for fuck's sake, they came up with us only last year, how has this happened?[38]) and consequently resting players with those play-off matches in mind.

Plus which, the other relegationists all face each other.

---

38 Ambition, managerial stability, and bankrolling businessman John Madejski, who hails from Stoke.

They have to lose points amongst themselves. How can it go wrong?

It's a rich man's world

For some time Pulis had been pursuing Ade Akinbiyi. It is possible that Ade has the word 'Striker' written on his passport in the box where occupation is stated, but many football fans would have a right good laugh if this was the case. Big Ade was out of favour at his latest home, Crystal Palace; in fact he had never been *in* favour there – the Palace supporters regarded him the worst forward they had ever signed by a mile. Ade had arrived at Palace direct from Leicester City, a Premiership club. Jack has a video called *Premiership Own Goals and Gaffs* which provides him, the massive, and me with hours of endless fun as we fast-forward and rewind again and again to watch top-class zillionaire defenders amaze their goalkeeping colleagues as they contrive to stick it into their own net from seemingly impossible positions; as those same goalkeepers in turn astound the defenders by allowing the ball to bobble through their legs when my granny could have saved it. The goalkeepers, in a routine I believe is a compulsory module at goalkeeper school, never fail but to give the imaginary offending divot of turf, in which the responsibility for their misfortune resides, the thousand-yard stare, and never fail to follow this up by carefully and disgustedly examining their studs, to make it clear to the crowd how it is that on this occasion the studs failed to function as studs are designed. It is stud-failure that has prevented them from moving like a goalkeeper ought to, which has resulted in them falling over and looking very silly indeed. It is nothing to do with them *personally*. In the sequence where strikers miss a sitter, landing it on the roof of the stand from a foot away, heading at the corner flag from six inches in front of an unguarded net, Ade has his own dedicated section.

It is a reflection of the expectations we were carrying for our full-time 'strike force' that, his well-publicized record notwithstanding, we were still lifted to a condition of mild anticipation at the prospect of the Big Man coming along to help us out. At a price. Here we had a character who had been disparaged left, right and centre, who could not score to save his life, who was being denied a starting place by a mid-table First Division team who were themselves on the road to nowhere, and who, amongst other complaints, was carrying a knee injury. Was it his record or his bill of health that was the stumbling block delaying his rumoured arrival? Neither. It was his contract. Still, some sort of arrangement is made and Ade becomes cover star[39] and centre-spread in the programme for

---

39 Bjarni was by now permanently dropped. A player called Mark Wilson came on loan from Middlesboro to occupy his position for a few games. The 'Boro fans view of Wilson was that he might possibly be a candidate from the reality TV show *Faking It*, whereby a person who is actually a vicar, for instance, attempts to pass himself off and hoax a panel of experts into believing, that, for example, he is an experienced used car salesman or a right winger. That's how dropped Bjarni was. Though the club kept tight-lipped about his situation, and the manager hedged whenever

the Wimbledon relegation game. Ade had made his debut against Rotherham, a match he limped out of with a hamstring pull to add to his other ailments, but his appearance that night meant that there were now pictures of him in our shirt, and these were put to immediate use. In the text accompanying the centre spread, Ade outlined his career to date. How's it been going then?

> In 1997 Gillingham bought me for a club record fee of £250,000 . . . the club were fantastic and so were the fans, but when Bristol City came in with a £1.2 million bid, another club record, it was in the interests of all parties concerned that I moved on . . . in 1999 Wolves signed me for £3.5 million and for the third time in my career I was signed for a club record fee . . . I moved, for yet another club record fee of £5 million, in 2000 to Leicester and couldn't wait to play in one of the best leagues in the world [the Premiership].

He intersperses this impressive financial history with his goal stats, which, while unexceptional, are okay – figures that support his case for being a top striker but only at Second Division level. His inability to deliver deteriorates to the point

---

questioned, the fact that a desperate end of season loanee was on the programme cover while Bjarni was the only first teamer never to have made it all year told its own story. They could have given him an issue just for the sake of double bluff, but then that would be PR.

of parody at Leicester, where, two divisions above his natural plateaux, he finds his limitations are not only cruelly laid bare, but also widely televised. Like many professional footballers (I have known one well enough to drink with, and I could say I was given an insight into how creatively their egos need to be managed in order for them to survive – favouritism, factions, cliques, cliques within cliques, gambling debts, infighting, unexplained droppings, injury-masking – it's no cakewalk, and I mean that) Ade sees himself in the best possible light, or to put it another way, he lives in Ade World, a land where the matter of most significance to him is his pecuniary value. Amounts that have been paid for him in his past inform the figures he will command in his future. Whoever emerges as the big payer will be where his loyalty lies, until the next one comes along. Fantastic fans – had to move on. Whatever.

Fantastic fans mean nothing to contemporary footballers. Business is business, and once you've crossed the white line on to the field of play the only other line that matters is the one at the bottom. Peter Ridsdale, the Leeds United chairman who oversaw £90 million worth of transfer spending during a couple of seasons at Elland Road, is on record as saying he has never known a group of people so interested in how much *more* money they can make than professional footballers, and he should know. Being entitled to 10 per cent of his cumulative signing-on fees (and a good agent will get you more), then based on his own figures Ade has banked a million in registrations alone. For not playing and not scoring, his Palace contract earned him £10,000 or so a week in wages. That was the price, that was the stumbling block. We made half a million from the Chelsea cup tie as everybody knows. Finally, in the light of this public knowledge, Pulis had managed to shame the board into coughing up this Ade-money for a few weeks. Because, from somewhere, and everybody knows this too, we must find a supplementary ability to hit the back of the net. Four goalless draws will not be enough to save us. Cookie's and Hookey's goals were their sixth and fourth of the season respectively, and neither will score again. It is this knowledge that allows our fans to welcome Big Ade – a comedy act with a record second to none at his extraordinary fee, an individual into whom £10 million pounds has been sunk and through whose person could be outlined the narrative of football's fiscal tailspin – as an agent of salvation. He takes to the field on his Saturday debut – one of four games in this season in which he will appear for us – kissing the club badge.

Billy no mates

The Wimbledon fans, due to their issues with their club, brought along a support numbering fifty-seven. We counted them. At this time the 'Western Alliance' was in Iraq, policing the world once more. One of the most arresting images I saw as a consequence of this activity was a photograph of a crowd watching a football match between two local sides in a stadium in Baghdad. The photograph was shot across the pitch at centre-line. Smoke from bombs and fires rose behind the stand in which about 400 Iraqi men were watching the game. This crowd was mainly gathered in a clump, but there were splinter groups and splinter groupettes and scattered on the edges there were a dozen blokes sitting on their own. For fuck's sake. I mean *come on*, there's a war going on behind you and a football match in front of you. You *must* have something to talk about.

The Wimbledon fans assembled in the same way: a (very) small group in the centre, then threes and twos and finally some singles out to the edges. Our away stand holds 4,000. Dwarfed by that, the grouped section looked lonely.

For some it must be the case that even Norwich City-style pockets of silence and Lacanian lapses into moments of freedom are not enough. They go to football matches simply to be away from it all, at peace with themselves, alone with their thoughts.

And on the third day we rose

Big Ade scored a goal against Wimbledon, a goal of outstanding quality, turning, spinning, taking out a couple of defenders and whacking it home top corner. That such a moment had been a long time coming for him was obvious: his joy was as unconfined as ours. Who cares what he costs? Sign him up: Ade for England. In winning the match we disposed of the team who had nothing to play for. It was Easter Saturday. Of course (how could it possibly be otherwise) Ade injured himself once more, and was unable to play two days later on Monday away to Coventry, who are absolute crap. We are no better than Coventry ourselves though, as the League table will testify, and even in the context of some of the utter garbage we'd seen earlier in the year, the first half against the Sky Blues (a shirt colour to rival yellow in the unsupportable shirt colour stakes) was the finished item insofar as an absence of quality is concerned.

Our seats were behind our 'Delilah' cheerleaders, the madmen who sing lines one and three. It goes without saying that they were the most entertaining aspect of the day, giving little lads from Coventry the cut-throat gesture in a pantomimic illustration of the fate that awaited them should they continue to sing rude songs at us or our team. This was *our* job as we barracked them off at the break, not something we like to do, their conviction is threadbare enough without that. But sometimes you have to be a True Supporter and give vent to your Honest emotions. After the barracking, I talked with the boss of the Delilahists, asking him why he chose the lines he used to set the song up. He went in for *At break of day when that man drove away I was waiting* as opposed to *I saw the light on the night that I passed by her window*. He explained that he'd experienced trouble with the *I saw the light* line, that for some reason it wasn't guaranteed to provide a successful intro, that TJ himself had had trouble with it, and they'd moved over to *At break of day* as it was simply more reliable, something to do with the scansion. I asked him what had happened to TJ, who I had not seen for some time. TJ is a mythical supporter, credited by some as the originating instigator of Delilah. I pretended I knew him, TJ, which I don't. This impressed Jack enormously, as I meant it to.

Oh he dunner come much now, the new boss of the Delilahists said, He's busy with his business. And of course, he's banned too, innee.

Is he? I said.

Oh yeah, the boss replied, We all are, he said, gesturing round at the Delilahistas. Once more in the proximity of legends Jack fell silent and attentive.

How d'you get in then? I asked. Meaning of course the Pikey ID cards.

He showed me his forged example. It's not hard to sort that out, is it, he said. I compared mine and his side by side. There was very little in it, though he had the prettier mugshot. Counterfeiting is an essential tool of survival when you're treated like a citizen of the Third World by the powers that be. And anyway, flashing my own card in my credit card wallet I had shown the stewards a picture of the top of my head only as I entered Highfield Road that day, so all they noted was some hair, and a frown. In real life I was wearing shades and a hat. Apart from the frown, I could have been anybody. By these means the scheme was beginning to settle down into something we could regard as normality. Because really, pre-match, while everyone's having a laugh and a joke and a Saturday, whose side are the stewards on, in the end? Sure, there are some Nazis amongst them. But they're not all like that. You'll find a way in.

Just into the second half, that wretched fellow Lee Mills, of the ex-Vale stock freak wonder goal at Norwich, was substituted for the last time. We rated him so highly by now that we sang *Time to go* to him as he left the field of play, the song normally reserved for the sendings off of opposing players. Big Chris Iwelumo took Mills's place to glorious cheers. You really do have to be a player of some Honesty to provoke that. With his first touch, Big Chris took a penalty. He hit it on to the post and, in a subliminal echo to Souleymane Oulare, it bounced out on to the arse of the forward-moving goalie and thence backwards into the net.

Mark Crossley, a loanee Premiership goalkeeper[40] on similar terms of remuneration to Big Ade, had stepped into Banks's boots in a further goalkeeping upgrade half-a-dozen matches back. He was already a candidate for player of the season as a consequence of crucial saves in those goalless draws in which I have claimed no shots were taken, and here he made a couple more crucial saves in a final twenty minutes that lasted for ever. There *were* shots in those goalless matches actually, always against us, moments I exorcised from my mind until the end of this match. When the whistle blew, I allowed such admissions space to exist, because by then I felt we might be safe. We beat

40 Godlike, handsome, suspect-on-crosses Cutler now found himself at the foot of the Third Division, palmed off on Swansea City. What sort of life is that? This is how and why I mean it when I say it's no cakewalk. My friend the professional footballer, who had been an under-21 for his country, was pensioned out of the game at the age of twenty-four with an irreparable groin injury. He began speculating about opening a restaurant, when in reality he could not make himself a slice of cheese on toast. An existential void of this nature is always there and waiting.

the team who are absolute crap 1–0. All other results went our way. At the fall of Easter Monday, Sheffield Wednesday and Grimsby had gone, were beyond salvation, were relegated, will visit Colchester United next year. We had taken six points from a possible six. We were fourth bottom, six points clear of Brighton who were third bottom. There were only two left to play. One more point and we would have done it, we would be saved. We only need one draw and Brighton have to win twice too. What are the odds on that?

The Ice Age

I hate Selhurst Park. It is a dreary ground, host to a dreary pair of clubs, has a supermarket integrated into the stand at one end and is a bastard to get to unless you are unfortunate enough to live there already, because otherwise you have to drive right across all the mankiest parts of south London, which are a permanent traffic jam, with an awful view of some horrible shops selling second-hand furniture. We arrived early because we could not sleep anyway and were having nightmares, but still we had to park. As we finally found a space an hour later, we were pounced on by two Icelandic gentlemen, a bald one and a bearded one who saw our colours and were eager to speak. Even in the light of our record there are Icelandic supporters who are willing to fly in from Reykjavik to watch us play. (!)

No, the bearded one says, when I put this to him, We've

come to see Spurs against Man United tomorrow, we've just come along here because we're in London.

Oh. But Icelandic people, they do care about Stoke City, generally?

Not really, he replies, There's not much interest in them back home to be honest.

Graham asks whether it wasn't the case that the Icelandics who *had* felt an involvement at the outset were really Gudjon-followers, that their interest had departed with him.

No no no! says the bald one. Gudjon is a madman, a complete maniac, out of his mind, a fool. Better now he's stopped drinking, but still insane. Everybody knows that.

I was warming to them.

'How d'you rate Bjarni?'

Good player, nice boy. How Gudjon had a decent son like that – and he's got two more besides! – is anybody's guess. What about this Pulis, why's he drop him?

Sub-Gudjon in the managerial-ability stakes is why.

Here we were, requiring a single point. I didn't give a stuff how we played and I was not alone. One point. That was all we wanted and that would be that. Had I been manager I'd have gone in for a 6–4 formation, six defenders and a four-man midfield. I mean, Ade was still re-injured, so how likely were we to score? Plus which we didn't need to. A goalless draw would suffice. And would suit all concerned, surely. Brighton, who *had* to beat Watford at home (which they did 4–0, the usual stitch-up, even the Watford manager admitted his players seemed to think they'd gone down to the south coast for a ride on the funfair) are Palace's deadly enemies. So why were the Palace fans cheering as news of the Brighton goals rained in? Because *we* were their visitors.

The truth is, though we have visited many a dump this season, we ourselves are an unglamour fixture of some standing. We are a no star opposition, thoroughly uncharming to the neutral eye, without, in the case of Palace, any particular history, and so devoid even of supporter hostility to enliven matters, though the Delilahistas had mobbed up and were singing *No surrender to the IRA* and other irrelevant ditties in attempt to help this situation along. At Coventry the week before they were as good as gold, confining themselves to pertinent football songs. They were entirely responsible for the atmosphere, such as it was. The Palace chairman, as is his commercial right, decided that he would have no truck with the Stoke City board's attempts to place constraints on his trade, refused to acknowledge the ID scheme and allowed anyone who wanted to pay cash on the day entry into his ground. As could be predicted, the PR coming out of *Pravda* all week denied that this would be the case, though a simple phone call to Selhurst Park would confirm it otherwise. This meant that the Delilahistas had swollen their numbers and were fuller of lager than usual for the awayday salvation party with lifted entry restrictions. Jack looked over at them. Heroic anti-establishment bandits, oppressed people like himself, yet on the other hand capable of turning on persons of his race at a moment's notice.

What, in the end, to make of this lot?

I was walking Ollie-the-lurcher around the University of East Anglia campus one evening some few weeks later. Trezza was at home checking this manuscript. No-football listlessness was at a high level, it being one of those summers without a World Cup or a European Championship to bridge the gap between seasons, but I would be picking Jack up after our walk to watch the England–Slovakia qualifier, at least, on television. I came across three lads, one of about ten, the other two a bit older. The university campus is bordered by woods and river and contains sports fields. It is popular with dog walkers and joggers. Ollie bounced over to the smallest of the boys (bouncing is Ollie's method of walking). The boy made to chase him. It was not an absolutely standard response of a boy to a dog, but it was nothing. A pair of middle-management joggers went past me. It was a warm night and they were shirtless in that faintly repulsive way of middle-aged men; while they were in reasonable muscular condition there was yet an inevitable looseness about their flesh. I had noticed them already, they were passing me for the second time. The three boys, their bikes lying on the ground, were hanging around the edge of a cricket pitch. Beside them was a small area of re-seeded grass which was cordoned off with flimsy netting. The smallest boy jumped the netting as the joggers went by. The taller of the two joggers admonished him, telling him to grow up. The boy said nothing but remained where he was within the netting. The jogger slowed and told him to clear off. There is a council estate near the university, and it was obvious that this was where the jogger meant him to clear off to. The boy and his mates grouped and swarmed but were going nowhere.

The jogger stopped, reversed his direction and moved towards the boys telling them once more to clear off, this time using the expression, Go on, fuck off you little shits. I was struck hard by the use of the word shits, a word in which the middle-managing jogger betrayed his world of assumption. These boys were scum who should not be allowed to share air with him in this arena, an arena over which neither he nor they nor I could claim any ownership whatsoever. I stopped. Ollie stopped. The three boys the dog and me formed a frozen still life as we faced him. A second elapsed. The jogger moved away. When he was at a safe distance the boys told him he could fuck off himself. The boys could look after each other, there had been no need for me to intervene beyond stopping, though I had continued walking as the situation developed in order to be on their side of the jogger before I made the stop. Because their side of the jogger was unquestionably the side I was on, even though I am a professional myself, who, in another life, might be a jogging middle-manager. This is how I put up with the excesses of the Delilahistas. It's a certainty that they've been on the butt end of the flaccid jogger's foul attitude all their lives. Their behaviour may be unacceptable sometimes, but my instinct to kick against the mentality of jogging middle-managers is overwhelmingly stronger than my instinct to disapprove of boys who jump fences.

Because as well as the bad song they start the good song:
She stood there laughing:
the week before we played 5–4–1

the week before that we played 4–4–2

and now here we were playing yet another formation, 5–3–2 with the two, the strikers, receiving no service whatsoever because the other eight had been briefed to do the one thing and only the one thing and nothing else are you listening there at the back?

Yes.

What did I say?

Defend, boss.

Right.

Defend. So what was the purpose of the two? Why not just isolate the one as had worked so successfully in our previous goalless draws? No one could possibly say. Palace were better than us and nicked a goal when we forgot to defend boss. We lost 1–0 to the team who would be happy to gift us a point. The Palace supporters delighted in our plight, though the only possible consequence of a repeat of this result-pattern next week in the final game would be the maintenance of First Division status for their deadly rivals, who had better goal difference. Maybe this fixture can be invigorated in future: *Outside, we'll see you all outside . . .*

I gunned the car home in a filthy mood having listened to Pulis telling the Five Live reporter that next week would be triffic, the sort of thing we fans look forward to: all the excitement of seeing whether we stay up or not. A world of his own, like Waddo, like all of them, it must be the only way they can survive.

If we lose next Sunday and Brighton beat Grimsby, who are already down, then Brighton will have pulled off the great escape and we will revisit Colchester. Even Graham was miserable, and Graham is of the blind optimist tendency, a person who will drive from Norwich to Anglesey at the bleep of a pager in the hope that the Black Lark will still be there when he arrives 400 miles later.[41] I just can't bear the idea of next week, he said, The tension, the baying when passes go astray, the crowd getting on their backs, all that.

When we were pounced on by the two Icelandic gentlemen earlier in the day, it had been the bearded one who asked *us* the first question.

'What do you make of the consortium?'

Cheerful and open, guests in my land, people I had met only a second earlier, making a solicitous enquiry as to how their fellow countrymen might be viewed. I could attempt diplomacy. But I had a bone to pick.

I think they're fucking wankers.

The bald one of the two laughed and nodded his agreement. Oh yes they are most certainly fucking wankers, he said, And they know fuck-all about football either.

No reply could have given me more enjoyment than this statement of the obvious, informed as it was by his local perspective, his inside knowledge, and confirming, as it did, the clear fact of the matter.

---

41 And it was too. The second ever spotted in Europe outside the 1993 Swedish sighting.

What *do* they know about? I asked.

Fish, the bald one replied, Fish and money.

And he went on to jibe at at the bearded one, who had lost a small fortune by investing in Stoke Holding.

How much?

Ooh . . . he stroked his beard and considered. The stock is down by about half, two-thirds, possibly.

They don't even know much about money, then? I said.

It was a rhetorical question, but the bearded one responded anyway. No, that's true.

This is a state of affairs that leaves them knowing only about fish.

This is a state of affairs that delivers us the terrors for the following seven days, not to mention the match itself.

It was all too easy

Radio Stoke had set up camp at the Britannia and were making a carnival-style outside broadcast on the Bank Holiday Sunday. We drove through the sunshine to the stadium listening to this jamboree. The mood coming over the airwaves could be summed up in the expression, These are the days we live for. The chief executive was on hand to offer the comment that it 'Wouldn't be Stoke' were it any other way, as if last-gasp matches spent desperately trying to avoid relegation directly back to the Second Division are somehow our birthright. Asked what the consequences of such a return would be, he replied that he had not given such an outcome any thought. You could say fair enough to that, that his answer was the sort of spin-dried positivity you'd expect to hear from the holder of his post prior to such a game. Something in his tone, though – that it was all a bit of a laugh and a joke – encapsulated the quaint, incoherent chaos of Stoke City perfectly. If the kind of forward planning that gave thought to outcomes such as immediate returns to the third tier of English football formed any part of the club's thinking, we might not find ourselves enjoying thrilling final day encounters attempting to avoid such a possibility. But then again, that wouldn't be Stoke. And maybe, actually, that's the way Stoke likes it.[42]

---

42 As stated elsewhere, it's mid-table mediocrity with nothing at stake that is our greatest fear. The relegation battle gave us everything to live for: we survived, we beat who the fucking hell are Reading 1–0 – a Big Ade header – and finally what Brighton did no longer mattered. Next season we will not have to play Rushden & Diamonds. Instead we will visit the Stadium of Light. Perhaps I should just shut up and be thankful that I support a team for whom, in another typical Stoke expression, There's never a dull moment.

Postscript: our handbags and our gladrags

After the final match, Jack and I went round to Old Stokie's for a cup of tea. Inside the domain of the legend, Jack sat quietly on a stool in the rapt posture I had come to expect in such company. In Old Stokie I believe Jack has added a member to his massive. OS is the paterfamilias, the Godfather. After sharing an embrace and our initial feelings – How are you? Drained; You? Knackered – I asked OS how he rated Pulis. He shook his head, and that was me too. The most important position at the club is team manager. The holder of this post is the public representation of ourselves. He is us. If I feel I've been harsh on Pulis, a person who did not get us relegated, I leave this thought: Stokies do not warm easily to the occupier of his position. To an extent this is the board's fault for never giving them anything to work with. But our natural insubordination comes into play too. We just don't like bosses. After the survival I overheard one bloke say this to another bloke:

Pulis? Complete tosser. But good manager.

I can't argue with that. Well, actually I can. But I'm not going to. Here is the absolute truth: he'll be gone one day and we'll all still be following Stoke. That is the fact.

An observation: post-Waddo we've had eighteen bosses, give or take a few caretakers, an average tenure of a year and three months a piece. It would surprise me to learn that this statistic is one that the board make available to applicants. You have to be a nutter and/or a desperado to take the job on (and the turnover rate compared to a triffic proper club barely needs pointing out). Of the eighteen, Lou Macari, who features twice in this reckoning, is the only one who we've warmed to. Many would say Gudjon was next behind him, but, as the late Peter Bromley put it of the Derby field trailing Shergar, So far back you'd need a telescope to see him. And all that Macari delivered, in as much as the record book will have it, was promotion from the Second to the First Division and an Autoglass Trophy, and to be honest, and though I cancelled a holiday to be at Wembley for the Autoglass, nobody counts that.

Why did we let Lou into our hearts?

There was this context: when he took over we had finished the previous season in our lowest ever Second Division position, our lowest ever League position (Alan Ball) and Lou reversed this slide. He unearthed Mark Stein, the Golden One, up there amongst our all-time favourite strikers. We played the sort of football people like to watch, and we had adventurettes in cup competitions. Which means we lost to Man United but emerged with credit. And Lou wasn't Mick Mills (mine eyes glaze over) or Joe Jordan (I expunge the memory from my hard drive). But, in dispassionate terms, Lou gave us not much, and nowhere near the top flight and the major domestic trophy that Waddo gifted us. Yet some would say we loved Lou even more. Why?

Old Stokie: Lou's case is a straightforward one. His character was of the 'loveable rogue' type. We all knew he was as bent as a five-bob note and had fingers in all the honeypots, but he had that difficult to define quality of being a leader. Given the circumstances, it's arguable that he was more popular than Waddo. I can never remember the singing of Waddo's name to the same degree as we did Lou's.[43] I was at the meeting in the King's Hall when he did a guest appearance. Over 2,000 people packed that hall for only one reason – Lou was there. Some people have a natural ability to engender loyalty. Lou had that for most supporters. Not all – but most. Perhaps his excellent work at Huddersfield is a pointer to his real ability as a manager. Despite having to sell most of his players, he did brilliantly in his season there, and when he left, they fell completely apart.

Yes, Lou was a good manager.

All I'd add is that Lou had the extra x-factor: in 'lovable rogue' OS defines the attribute we are obliged to rate most highly in a Stokie. He needed to be as bent as a five-bob note and to have his fingers in all the honeypots in order to connive any co-operation out of the pricks in the boardroom. Don't we all. In achieving this he allowed us to be reminded of ourselves at our best.

I imagine an Austin Maxi would have been as much as he needed to impress the ladies.

---

43 *Lou lou skip to my lou; Lou lou skip to my lou; skip to my Lou Macari*: the sweetest song any rogue could have bestowed upon him.

Other business

After twenty games and 3 [three] victories, Lt Steve Cotterill was dismissed, along with Sgt Wilko, from his post at Sunderland. On the Saturday following this sad news, the Saturday of Peter Hoekstra's Turner Prize winning goal, we celebrated by singing the modern classic:

He's on the dole, he's on the dole,
he's on the,
Cotterill's on the dole

to the tune of *Football's Coming Home*. Sunderland's relegation to the First Division was with the lowest points gained and least goals scored in the Premiership's history. Cheltenham, from whence Cotterill came, were also relegated, from the Second back to the Third. Like Stoke, these teams both play in red and white. We broke the Cotterill jinx by being the only club who played in these colours and who had been touched by the Quitter's magic to end the year in the same division in which we had begun it.

Days after their relegation Brighton began a revenge campaign. The *Guardian* reported an extraordinary plan by East Sussex and Brighton & Hove councils to dump waste in holes in the ground of less prosperous areas. The plan would involve lorries carrying rubbish collected from doorsteps in Brighton and the South Downs on 450-mile round-trips to Stoke-on-Trent where the stuff could be buried.

Bjarni Gudjonsson left Stoke City on the final day of the season. Jack hung around outside after the match, and in a curious mixture of the wide-eyed innocent and the budding ironist he collected the whole team's autographs – the good, the bad and the indifferent – on the cover of his *Oatcake*. I have not solicited a footballer's autograph since I was his age, but on seeing Bjarni I borrowed Jack's *Oatcake* and collected his signature again, on the back cover. I did this in order that I could say this:

I think it's a disgrace the way you have been treated.

Bjarni had a small mob about him, and was signing diffidently without eye-contact. He raised his glance at my remark and looked me straight in the eye and said nothing. I took this to mean: I completely agree with that assessment.

Whatever the politics of his scapegoating, you will struggle to find any sane person who thinks he was pushed out of the club because he was not the best right winger we had available.

He was immediately signed up by Bundesliga side VfL Bochun where he will join his brother Thordur.

West Ham United, Jack's new Premiership team, had as miserable a campaign as us – we'll be playing them as well as

STEPHEN FOSTER

Sunderland in the coming season. Tracking another poor side helped him not a bit: he will stick to supporting just the one basket-case in future. We will, though, have a new top-flight outfit to follow; we are nominating VfL Bochum of the Bundesliga as our second team.

Steward of the Year: the one at Norwich City who asked me where Stoke was and if it was far away. Light years, I would've said, if I was quick enough. I contented myself with a geographical explanation which meant nothing to him.

Column of the Year: Richard Balls' 'Fan's Eye' in the *Eastern Daily Press*. Richard never quite got over the loss of points involved in Norwich's slip-up at home to Lowly Stoke. He cited the game often as the pivotal moment in the decline of the Canaries' season. On one occasion, weeks after the match, there was even an accompanying picture of our players celebrating the victory, sorry, draw. Kept my spirits up.

Speed Camera of the Year: slyly tucked round a bend on the east-bound A14 near Milton Keynes.

Phrase of the Year: Speed camera coming up round this bend. (Graham Etherington)

Distance of the Year: the gap between our custodians and us.

Sour of the Year: the one where Graham stood up out of the sunroof in his replica shirt giving the Vs and terrifying young children on the back of a school bus.

Sweet of the Year: Megabeans.

Fan of the Year: the old lady at the back of Turf Moor who had been driven to madness by years of StokeLife. She stood there screaming the names of the class of '72 – C'mon Ritchie, C'mon Greenhoff, C'mon Pejic, Terry Conroy on the wing. Hair-raising.

Bare stats:
Victories witnessed: 10 (missed 2)
Draws witnessed: 14
Losses witnessed: 17 (missed 3: only counting 2 – banned from Millwall)
Miles driven: 11,800
Cost: You can't put a price on this.

STEPHEN FOSTER

Oatcake messageboard contributors have, knowingly and unknowingly, helped me through my mood swings, depressions, and suicidal feelings via the exchange of crap jokes, bad attitudes, temper tantrums, hissy fits, mis-information and wholly erroneous transfer/loan speculation. Rumour, hearsay, gossip, slander, defamation, character assassination and libellous comment have all been of great assistance. Interlectewal and emergancy spelins should also be acknowledged alongside ludicrous claims, nonsensical asides, insane suggestions, utter and total bollocks [ERROR: Bad Language], outright horseshît and not forgetting informed opinion, critical analysis and sometimes, even, actual boring facts and stuff like that.

So, in no particular order, thanks to:

TEL2U OldStokie Norwich_Stokie plymptonpotter grey_man MCF_74 GuernseyDave Will_75 OldStokiesson ghettostokie SA_78 djh68 skip_rat Paddock PMac IlfordDave Blanca Joe_in_oz spiderpuss DOPEYJOE SuperStokie LeicsPotter MysticPotter gudjonisgod ParaPsych Fran_SCFC Alli_G The_Gin_Soaked_Boy potters11 mart_72 shedload_for_ginger Boz_the_Stokie SuperBjarni StokeMark JR_Nantwich SurreyStokie KidderminsterPotter Bristol_Mick LouieIsTheKing PenkvillePotter Not_Nick_Hancock maucek Archie_Pelago Pricey_SCFC Boothen_EndDave pez_75 gingist 1STEINO Robo10_Stoke Klute portsmouthpotter jimmygscfc Stripey HelpfulHenry Log_of_Leeds Broughsie Linx Trondheim Davef Spuddy_Magoo dave_hexham AndyK ron_at_norwich Alloallocop redcar-stokie whalleyrangepotter wrenburystokie Clan2

Macc loz115 GCsdf thetop chop_lad Ramo craig67 addlestonestokie Oatcaker anewman jpm1964 123sc johnnyb_scfc Smari Manchestermalc tc_on_the_wing lars_norm TheWiseMaster StavangerSteve Dobber utch OnlyoneNigelGleghorn DaveJohnno cambs_stokie Greenacre JimmyGrimblesBoots tommytrinder DavidY maidstonestokie Frenchie mattyb_scfc_2 chell_rosey Greebo fatgazzer dan_mase steph51 VofS MikR kevalb scfc_mica Kewstokie PJnotTJ ange81 surbiton_stokey Happylarry NewGlennA macca100 robbo_w HankHank stokie_nick bigbazza winchester_stokie Merseyside_Potter Stokecity2k1 bigdave1 Smiler_Andy Aldershot_stokie basti Moosehead Mr_Flirty onewaynebiggins FarmersPoetry birly larry_potter gudjon1 knowles IverPotter NOFX_Potters ukyestony parksy Ryd67 leedspotter Braintree_Rex presthaven dave8 Heidar Kenilworth_Stokies Rock_Ape stevie68 small_fry Dazasson rednwhitecardie Romford_Stokie petemac kevkj Suffolk_Potter potter16 its_me_Hoody mafr cartwright4 TokyoJoe Chinaski Gunslinger nellbell Rex_The_Ref simon_stainrod figsy beachboydave Tomjoneslovechild delilah 987scfc spiderpuss Norters padders01 GermanStokie Trouserdog Bjorn coll40 bruges_exile JooolZ northstokie ant_thefire RipRoaringPotter Andy_is_a_STOKIE colmanspig sokrates BillyBluebird Gods Neutron AuntyRuthsWig OohICouldCrushAGrape TapeLoops houstonmike Albert_Tatlock apologies2_ aneone leftout forgotten injured or_changed username ForPersonal or_LegalReason

Special mention for Smudge_SCFC. Unbiased match reporter, site editor and philosopher.

GOOAAARRRRRRRRRNNNNN STOKE!!!